MW00781338

NOT
ENOUGHNESS™

NOT
ENOUGHNESS™

THE GIFT AND THE CURSE

JAREK TADLA

Author Photograph by Onzyte Productions
Cover Layout by Cledis Duran
Book design and production by Tami Boyce

Published by Niche Pressworks
Indianapolis, IN

ISBN : 978-1-962956-40-6 Hardback
978-1-962956-29-1 Paperback
978-1-962956-30-7 eBook

Library of Congress Cataloging-in-Publication Data on File at lccn.loc.gov

This book is dedicated to all of the men who have lost their lives to suicide and to the families they left behind and to those who are struggling with depression and suicidal thoughts today. You are not alone. There are people who can help you.

Also, to my children, for being my rock and my purpose.

TABLE OF CONTENTS

ADDICTED TO THE PURSUIT

DOWNWARD SPIRAL

The sun was shining. The birds were chirping. It was a beautiful day in South Florida — the kind of day northerners travel thousands of miles to experience.

Or maybe it wasn't. It could have been 50 degrees, gray, and drizzling for all I knew. The thick, velvet drapes were closed, so none of the Florida sunshine could make it into the room. Plus, I kept the light off most of the time, so it was always dark.

I was in bed, trapped in a relentless fog of despair. For the last forty-four days, I had been anchored to this very spot — my master bedroom. And somehow, I couldn't break free from this dismal, oppressive place. No matter what I did, I couldn't figure out how to pull myself out. And the whole time I was there, this voice just kept repeating over and over, "You're not good enough. Nobody cares about you. Nothing you've done means anything to anyone." It was a whisper in my head that I couldn't drown out.

Logically, I knew what the voice was saying wasn't true. I've done so many things in my life. I'm a successful businessman. I'm an athlete — an Ironman. I've made multi-millions. And when it comes to people who care about me, I've got so many. Logically, I had so much worth living for.

But depression doesn't listen to logic. It listens to that devil's voice whispering in your ear. He can be very persuasive. No matter how much you've done, he tells you it's not enough. No matter how many people love you, he tells you you're unlovable. He repeats it over and over and over, drowning out every other thought until you can't help but believe it.

And over time, the fact that I HAD done so much in my life became part of the depression. "You think you've accomplished so much, but just look at you," the devil's voice would say to me. "You can make a billion dollars, but you can't even get yourself out of bed? Pathetic. How could anybody ever love someone like that?"

It became a vicious circle. Depression kept me from doing anything. But then I had anxiety over not doing anything, which led to self-hatred over being lazy. The self-hatred, in turn, led to more depression. By the time I realized what a deep hole I'd let myself get into, I was in too deep to do anything about it.

It finally reached the point where I didn't want to live anymore. But at the same time, killing myself was something I didn't have the energy for.

Obviously, I couldn't do it in the house, where Jessica or my kids or someone else I cared about might find my body. I'd never do that to them. So, instead, I thought about taking my boat out into deep water, far away from everything and everyone, with my scuba gear, employing the benefits of "nitrogen narcosis," which can produce severe disturbances of consciousness and even loss of consciousness, leading to death. But it's a peaceful death. I thought that might be the perfect plan. No one would know what happened to me. It would be my final deep dive.

But in order to do that, first, I'd have to load all of my gear into the boat. I'd have to get up out of bed and leave the room. And that was more than I could manage.

I was too lazy even to kill myself. What a loser. So, I stayed there, day after day, with the devil's voice on a constant loop, for forty-four days.

JESSICA

On this particular Wednesday morning, though, something different happened. The bedroom door suddenly opened, and a stream of light from the hallway pierced my self-imposed darkness as Jessica walked into the room.

I rolled over to avoid any potential conversation.

"Enough!" Jessica declared. "You need to get out of bed."

I had started out with a good reason for being in bed. A few weeks before that day, I'd been laid out with the flu. Suffering from fever and congestion and feeling terrible, I had crawled into bed and then didn't do anything for a couple of days.

But it's amazing how fast a day or two can become a week or two. And then, just as fast, a week or two can become four weeks or six. Before long, I was in bed all the time.

For all my kids and employees knew, I was just sick. I'd heard of people who had long COVID. Let them believe that was it.

I used that as my excuse for being a walking zombie. The truth was, I wasn't sleeping at night because the intrusive, depressive thoughts wouldn't leave me alone. It felt like the worst hangover ever, day after day. Except that I haven't had a drink for years. And the feeling wouldn't leave.

So, when my kids were over, I'd just surf through the day, trying to get by, trying to get through, doing the bare minimum. When my kids weren't there, I never even left my room — dark and dismal, with the lights off and the curtains drawn.

And then Jessica opened the curtains. And it pissed me off.

A LONG-OVERDUE CONVERSATION

"What the heck?!" I groaned, squinting at the sudden stream of sunlight invading my personal space.

She marched across the room, yanked the sheets back, and grabbed me by the heels, pulling me from the bed. I was too weak to fight her off.

"You need to get out of bed," she repeated. "You can't go on like this."

"Go away!" I snapped. "I'm sick!"

"It was weeks ago that you were sick," she said.

"Go away!" I shouted again. Who did she think she was, doing this to me?

"A lot of people are worried about you," she said. "I'm worried about you."

"Just leave me alone!" I shouted. "Why are you still here?" In the moment, I meant, *Still here in our room when I keep telling you to go away.* But there was also the underlying meaning. A lot of people WOULD have left by now. Left completely, and for good.

She could easily have started the conversation with, "I'm sick of your issues, and I'm moving out." But she never said that.

Instead, she said, "**Because you don't leave people just because they're going through something.**"

"I'm fine!" I told her.

"You're not fine," she replied. "I can see it. I've seen you like this before. You're not going there again."

"Yeah, what do you care?" I asked.

No — I didn't just ask. I yelled. I screamed. The devil that had been whispering toxic things in my ear for two months didn't take kindly to being confronted and started lashing out. But Jessica didn't waver.

"You've helped so many people. But right now, you can't even help yourself." When she said that, I felt like she'd punched me in the gut. She was right, and I knew it. I didn't want to face it, but she was about to make me do just that.

"So many people look up to you," she continued. "And you're just lying in bed all day."

THE BIG LIE

"YOU'VE HELPED SO MANY PEOPLE. BUT RIGHT NOW, YOU CAN'T EVEN HELP YOURSELF." WHEN SHE SAID THAT, I FELT LIKE SHE'D PUNCHED ME IN THE GUT.

Yes. So many people looked up to me, and yet I was trapped in this hole I'd dug for myself. I was surrounded by family and friends and people who loved me, and yet I felt so alone.

While I'd been shut up in my room, I'd been without any real, meaningful human interaction. That isn't to say I wasn't talking to people. As I said, I had plenty of friends and family who cared about me and would do anything for me if I only asked. But how could I ask? How could I let them see what a failure I'd become — the person they loved and cared about? I felt like that wasn't me. And if I let them see the real me, they'd realize it was someone they could never love — only pity.

It was like drowning in a three-foot-deep pool. All I had to do was stand up and breathe, but I was too weak to do it. I couldn't reach out to the people who could help me, even though they were right beside me.

Jessica was literally right beside me, sleeping next to me the whole time. And my kids were there every other week. Not to mention friends and family who would call.

And, of course, Raul. Raul is my personal development coach. He's there to make sure, well, among other things, that things like this don't happen. I call him weekly to check in and talk about how I'm doing. I knew if I didn't, he'd be on my case. So, I'd make the calls faithfully, as scheduled. And I would lie.

"Yes, Raul, things are great here. Doing well. Keeping busy." And so on. I'd tell him whatever he wanted to hear, just to get off of the call and be done for another week. Raul is the person I pay specifically to keep me from slipping down into this dark place. He's amazing at what he does, but as they say, you can lead a horse to water, but you can't make him drink. He couldn't force me to get better. I had to ask for help.

The lie was easier.

That's the way it was with anybody who called. I'd talk for a few minutes, or I'd put on my "sick voice" to let them know I wasn't up for making plans. But all the while, I was thinking, *When will this be over?* until I could hang up.

It was exhausting trying to be the version of me that everyone else expected me to be. I couldn't keep it up for more than a few minutes at a time. I didn't have the energy anymore.

So, I lied and told everybody I was fine. I thought I had them all fooled.

Except, of course, I didn't. They all knew something was up. It's just that nobody had the guts to say it to my face. Nobody except Jessica. In fact, the main reason everybody knew something was wrong with me was because Jessica had told them.

During those weeks, she'd called Raul and some of my other friends to let them know I was going through something and ask them to call and try to help me. But I wouldn't listen to any of them. In the end, the only one who was able to pull me out was Jessica.

With the gut punch she'd just given me, Jessica finally convinced me to get out of the room. After forty-four days in bed, I finally got up. I went to the living room and immediately lay down on the couch. It was a small move, but it was a start.

AT LAST, THE LIGHT

I'd had the house I was living in at the time specially built. The living room was designed to look like the lobby of a luxury hotel. It had a big, wide-open space and 50-foot ceilings. And at the very top was a skylight. I eased reluctantly out of my bedroom fortress and into the wide-open living room, where I looked up through the square opening.

I froze, in awe of what I saw. *That's beautiful,* I said to myself.

It was the first positive thought I'd had in weeks. I couldn't take my eyes off the view through the skylight.

I watched the white clouds moving through the blue sky. They moved so quickly. They'd blow by, and before you knew it, they were gone, just like my life. It moved so fast, and it would be over before I knew it. And I was spending every day of it in a darkened room, not doing anything or talking to anyone.

Man, I thought. *I've got to get out.*

Flipping the Switch

The decision to start living again was like flipping a switch. One minute, I was plotting how I could end my life. The next minute, I knew I had to get out; I had to come back. That's how change happens for me.

It was the same when I made the decision to stop drinking. I was waiting for a flight at the airport. One minute, I was thinking, *Let me get another beer before I get on the plane.* But by the time I was on the plane, I was texting all of my friends, saying *I'm done with drinking.* When we landed, I had a whole lot of replies with mixed reactions. But by that time, I knew I was done.

So yeah, making the decision is easy. But following through is *hard.* Getting out of the hole takes a lot longer than getting into it. When it came to getting out of the room and out of my depression, Jessica and I took it slowly.

Day one, I got out of my dark bedroom and into the living room to see the blue sky. Day two, I finally went outside. It was only to the driveway, but it was still a struggle. That little way was all I could manage, and it made me realize just how bad I had let myself get. But at least I was making progress. Baby steps.

That first day, Jessica got me out of bed. The second day, I got out of bed myself. Honestly, I did it mainly to avoid another confrontation with her. But still, whatever works. Whatever gets you out.

The Long Road Back

I'd fallen into depression over a period of three or four days, and I'd been in bed for two months. But climbing out of the hole and getting back to where I was before that took a good six months. And even then, it wasn't a matter of "getting over it." Honestly, it took those six months just to realize how bad things had really been.

I feel much better now than I did then, and I've resumed my regular, active lifestyle, but the journey never ends. I'm still a work in progress. I still struggle sometimes, and I still have to work to keep from drifting back into the dark — back into the room.

TELLING MY STORY

So, how did I get to this point? I mean, I had everything — cars, houses, money in the bank, and, of course, my kids, and Jessica, my queen. I was on top of the mountain. And I still managed to find myself in that deep pit of despair and depression. When I realized that, it was a revelation. If it could happen to me, it could happen to anybody.

I said that my friends, despite my best efforts, all knew there was something wrong with me. But no one was willing to say anything. No one wanted to talk about it, and that only served to keep me in the room longer.

It was Jessica's decision to confront me that finally got me out. And once I'd turned that corner, **I made the decision to tell my story**. I'd tried to shut my friends out, but now I wanted to share with them what I'd gone through and how I had struggled. And I saw how sharing what had happened to me helped them with their own struggles. That was the ah-ha moment.

The Void of Success

If you're hoping to find out how I made all of my money or to learn a bunch of business secrets that will turn you into a millionaire or a billionaire, that's not what this book is. I could tell you all about my rise to the top, the deals I've made, and how they've paid off. But that's not what this book is for.

First off, there are plenty of other books that will give you those tips if that's what you're looking for. But ask yourself this: Why do you want a billion dollars at all? Money isn't a goal in itself. It's a means to an end. So, what is it you want that you think a billion dollars will help you to get? Houses? Yachts? Vacations?

More to the point, what would you do all day once you had those billion dollars? Would that be enough? Would you be satisfied? Would you be happy? Likely as not, you'll still have that void in your life. Only now you'll need to find some other way to fill it.

There's no worse feeling than feeling incomplete. That nagging feeling that something is missing eats away at you and won't leave you alone. If you can't get rid of it, all you can do is numb it.

That's why we find ways to sedate ourselves — so the pain will go away.

Different people numb themselves differently. You can use drugs, alcohol, sex, gambling, food... Or you can do like I did and find something that looks on the surface like success.

That's what this book is about. Not the success that I had but the lessons I learned on that journey about coping with the problems life throws at you. I'm going to share 10 of those lessons with you: things I learned but forgot during those two months in bed.

Through every journey I had, it seemed on the surface that I was successful. I accomplished great things.

But there was always a lie underneath it. **The lessons I'm sharing here are the truths I learned by confronting those lies.**

Relearning those lessons finally got me out of bed and to a new level of myself — someone who can finally feel complete. I'm still working on these lessons, and I always will. *But in the meantime, I want to share them, both the good and the bad, for anyone who's struggling in the darkness. If you are in that frame of mind, I hope this book finally helps you back into the light.*

"NOT ENOUGHNESS"

It took me a while to come up with a way to describe what I was dealing with. At first, it seemed to revolve around the idea of money.

I've shown you the truth of that old cliché, "Money can't buy happiness." In a way, I've lived that truth.

But the thing is, my focus was never on *having* money. It was about *making* money. Making those deals and chasing that next big score. That was my cocaine. I struggled with drugs and alcohol for a long time, but at my core, I was addicted to the pursuit.

So yeah, I had everything I wanted; a yacht, a jet, beautiful houses all over the world, luxurious vacations, I could go anywhere I wanted for the rest of my life. But at the same time, my pursuit of money drove my friends and family away. I never saw my kids because I was working all the time. I let two marriages fall apart. I destroyed the things that I cared about, trying to make money. Why?

I was trying to get rid of that feeling that constantly haunted me — that feeling of Not Enoughness.

Not Enoughness is the pain of feeling like no matter what you do, you will never be enough. That's the core of it. You can make your billion dollars, you can have your "success," but you'll still feel it. Because it's not about *having* enough or *doing* enough, it's about *being* enough.

You find yourself obsessed with pursuing external validation, but what you're really doing is trying to fix an internal emptiness.

I know about the feeling of Not Enoughness all too well. I've dealt with it my whole life.

THE BIG LIE – "YOU ARE NOT ENOUGH"

THE FIRST ABYSS

I grew up in Poland. If you've ever been to Poland, you know there's plenty to like about it. It can be a beautiful place, with any number of areas worth seeing. What I don't recommend is growing up there during the last decades of the Cold War. My childhood there was dark, cold, and bleak, and the culture I grew up in was unforgiving.

Poland was never officially part of the USSR, but the governing party was firmly under Soviet control. That situation meant we were also poor, with little opportunity to excel, advance, or make anything of ourselves other than what our families had been for generations.

So essentially, what I'm saying is long before Jessica opened the curtains and got me out of my room, I had to pull myself out of a different hole.

Dulling the Pain

The culture that develops in a bleak and rough place tends to be bleak and rough as well. The people I grew up with were devoid of empathy. Alcohol was as common as water. Lots of folks drank. It was what they did to dull the pain.

My father was strict, and he made it clear every day that nothing I did would ever be good enough for him. If I did poorly in school, he'd challenge me for not doing well. If I did OK in school, he'd challenge me for not doing better. If I did well in school, he usually thought that I probably cheated to do that well.

My mother made excuses for his behavior. "You know how hard he works." "You can't antagonize him like that." "He just wants what's best for you." So, the cycle of a home "void of empathy" ensued.

When she said those things, all I heard was, *"It's OK that your father is rough on you."* And *"It's your fault that your father is so rough."* And ultimately just, *"You are Not Enough."* If I was Enough, my father wouldn't act that way. If I was Enough, we wouldn't be so sad all the time. Or we'd have more money.

Well, I could do something about at least one of those things.

I owe a lot of my success to my father. Love and encouragement can be good motivators, but for my money, nothing makes a person so driven as pure spite.

My memory of growing up in Poland was more the darker realities: the soot from the local coal factories that left our clothes darker and dirtier, the reality of the political climate, the actual climate. I remember being physically disciplined in school and then again at home, as I mentioned. This was the usual case for children seeking attention with bad behavior.

If you had asked me then about my father, I would have characterized him as tough and strict. I understand now that he was what he had been taught to be through generations of men who do not show love through a "soft" approach, especially to their sons. Ironically, as an adult, it was this harshness that fueled my desire to work hard and succeed at all costs but also left me feeling like none of it was ever enough.

As a child, I resented him for not allowing me to be less, for expecting so much out of me, for making me feel like second place was not acceptable. I understand now, as a man and as a parent, that this was his way of holding me accountable and pushing me to be great at WHATEVER I did for the rest of my life.

DESPERATELY TRYING TO BE ENOUGH

I started my entrepreneurship journey at age ten. I went around the neighborhood collecting cans and glass bottles and saving up the money. When I was a little older, I started taking odd jobs: raking leaves, shoveling walkways, whatever I could find that would put a few extra dollars in my pocket — mine and nobody else's.

I hardly ever spent it. Most of what I made, I hid away. I was saving up for what I really wanted — to finally make my escape.

Earlier, when talking about my conversation with Jessica, I mentioned the devil who had been whispering toxic things in my ear for the last two months. That's not entirely accurate. He'd been there a lot longer than that. The toxic voice started while I was collecting those cans and bottles.

The work was my driving force. At home, nothing I did was ever enough. But if I could make money, if I could succeed where my parents failed, then maybe I *would* be Enough. I could be better than my father, and I would prove him wrong. Seeking anything that would prove my dad wrong is what drove me from collecting cans and bottles at 10 years old to retiring at 28.

And I just kept chasing it. Because no matter how hard I worked, no matter how much success I saw, no matter how much money I made, I still felt like I was Not Enough. But if success was the goal, then work was the means. So, whenever I felt like I was Not Enough, I retreated further into my work. It was an escape. I told myself I was working.

All I was really doing was avoiding, just like you might do with drugs or alcohol or porn or whatever else. It was the only way to silence that devil that kept whispering in my ear: "Jarek, you are Not Enough."

THE TRUTH – YOU ARE ENOUGH

THE VOICES CAN'T SWIM

Work and spite weren't the only things that drove me. Another thing I used to fill the void was sports. I got into swimming at a very young age. And when I say, "got into," I mean that if I wasn't working, sleeping, or in school, I was swimming. I would swim for hours. Swimming became my first real addiction.

Much like working and making money, exercise as an addiction looks on its surface like a good thing. Like working and making money, it's a means to an end. If your goal in exercising is to get healthy, feel better physically, and maintain an active lifestyle, that's great.

But if, like with me, you're using exercise to drown out the pain you're feeling inside and to silence the devil who's whispering in your ear, then it becomes a problem. And since it's a problem people will congratulate you and give you awards for, moving past it isn't an easy task.

It also didn't help that swimming became a way to spite my father.

It didn't start out that way. In the beginning, I took up swimming for me. The ritual of it and the rhythm of the strokes back and forth across the pool were almost hypnotic. Everything disappeared in the water. There were no school assignments I wasn't doing well enough on. There were no cans and bottles to collect.

In fact, the more I swam, the harder it became to berate me. I was 6'2" with a swimmer's body — nothing but lean muscle. I was fast, I was strong, I was tireless. I wasn't someone you wanted to mess with. Unless you were my father.

SECOND PLACE

I still remember coming home one day after a swim meet. I'd been swimming competitively for maybe a year or two at that point, and I was already one of the best. I walked through the door with my medal around my neck, grinning ear to ear. And then I heard my father's voice.

"So, you won, then?"

"I got second place!" I happily reported.

"Second place? You're this happy about second place?" he grumbled.

"It's a huge swim meet!" I protested. "Some of the best swimmers in the region were there!"

"Best swimmers in the region?" my father scoffed. "Well, clearly, you're not one of them."

"But I got second place!" I repeated.

"What are you practicing five hours a day for, day in and day out, if you're only going to come in second?" My father's words still echo in my mind. "Sounds to me like you lost."

THE ULTIMATE GOAL

After that, I trained harder, swam longer, and put every ounce of strength into shaving seconds off my time. No more second place. No more second best. My father's criticism had burned into my brain, and the water was the only thing that could drown it out.

I competed, I won, I swam some more. Repeat. For years. Until finally, I had a chance to swim my way to Seoul.

The 1988 Summer Olympics were in Seoul, Korea. It was everything I'd dreamed of. Not just in terms of swimming success. Qualifying for the Olympics meant I'd finally made it!

But the devil, whispering in my ear, didn't go away. All the while I trained with the rest of the Olympic team, one phrase just kept echoing in my head: *What are you practicing for?*

It was my father's taunt to me, but it was also a legitimate question. What WAS I doing all of this for? Swimming had been my whole life for upwards of a decade, but why? I used to enjoy it. But now I was just doing it to prove something. I used to do it to drown out the voices of Not Enoughness. But now, the voices had returned. No matter how hard I practiced or how much I succeeded, all I could hear was my father's voice, telling me I was still Not Enough. And if I could qualify for the Olympics and still be Not Enough, then would anything ever be Enough?

"Only a silver medal?" I imagined him saying to me. *"All that work, and you couldn't even bring home the gold? Sounds to me like you lost."*

A NEW DREAM

The truth was swimming wasn't my dream and hadn't been for a long time. It was my father's dream for me. I didn't enjoy it. I was just chasing something that I would never have. And so, in that moment, I made a decision. I walked away from the Olympic team and chose not to go to Korea.

It was the opportunity of a lifetime, and I threw it away. I still wonder sometimes if maybe I made a huge mistake. I came that far. I got an opportunity most people only dream of. Should I at least have seen it through? What path would I have gone down if I had competed — win or lose?

But in the end, even if it was a mistake, I stand by it. Why? Because it was my first real attempt at seeking freedom. It was my declaration, not just to my father but to myself, that I was in charge of my own destiny. I wouldn't let someone else tell me where I had to go or what I needed to do to be considered a success. I wouldn't let anyone else tell me I'm Not Enough.

WHAT CAN YOU ACHIEVE?

Yes, it's possible that I could have won the Olympics and taken home a gold medal and a thousand new opportunities. But I walked away because I realized something for the first time in my life: **What you're told and believe is what you become.**

The whole world, including teachers, coaches, priests, family, and friends, made me feel "less than," so I became less than on the inside. Even qualifying for the Olympics didn't change that. The only way out was to tell myself something better. Not to prove my value but to see my value and ground myself in that. I needed to learn to love myself, not for what I could be or what I might be, *but for what I am.*

> **I NEEDED TO LEARN TO LOVE MYSELF, NOT FOR WHAT I COULD BE OR WHAT I MIGHT BE, *BUT FOR WHAT I AM.***

Who knows what I could have done in the Olympics? But the fact is, I'd already proven I had the grit and determination and drive to achieve anything. I proved that before I qualified for the Olympics. I proved it even before I walked through the door years earlier with my second-place medal. I've proven it to myself every day, over and over.

So why use that grit and determination and drive just to prove myself again to someone who would never see my worth? If I know I can achieve anything, I'd rather do something much more difficult but much more valuable: inner work. The work it takes not just to sedate that devil's voice or drown it out but to get rid of it entirely.

Without really knowing it, I started doing that even back then, when I was a young kid. And I've continued it for more than 20 years, consciously or subconsciously. It's not been an easy road, and as you've already seen, there have been more than a few setbacks. And there may be more yet to come. But for now, the devil's voice is silent. And in its place, something else whispers in my ear, in the voices of all of those who love me: "**Jarek, you are Enough.**"

GETTING COMFORTABLE WITH BEING UNCOMFORTABLE

WHEN IT ALL CAME TUMBLING DOWN

It was late in the evening, around 2007. I was sitting in my office at home, going through papers and muttering to myself. I'd slept in the office the night before and most nights that week, and I probably would again tonight.

Well, "slept" isn't entirely true. I wasn't actually sleeping much at all, and I was barely eating. I spent all my time going through reams of papers and files, trying to squeeze something out of them and coming up empty again and again.

"Dang it!" I yelled at the bank statement in front of me and slammed it down on the desk.

Then, from the other room, I heard the voice of my six-year-old daughter.

"Mommy?" she asked my then-wife. "Why is Daddy always so upset?"

The Crash

The housing crash took most people by surprise. But me? I'd been preparing for it for years. I didn't know when it was going to happen, obviously, but I knew there had to be one at some point. And I knew that if you're ready for it, there's a lot of money to be made when the bottom drops out.

So, in 2001, I started buying property. I went to foreclosure sales to get buildings dirt cheap. I bought up as much as I could. And to get the money for these deals, I borrowed. A lot. I borrowed from banks, from friends, from business associates, and wherever I could get it. I wasn't worried. The buildings generated a steady income, and the income paid off my debts.

Then came the Lehman Brothers crash.

The crash itself didn't hurt me too much. Like I said, I'd been preparing for this. The problem was that the people I'd been borrowing money from weren't OK. A lot of people lost a lot of money. So, the first thing they started to do was call in their debts. I started hearing from everybody.

"Jarek, I need $30,000 back." Not a problem.

"Jarek, I need $100,000 back." A little bit of a squeeze, but I could make it work.

"Jarek, I need $1,000,000 back." Then it became a problem. I didn't have that or anything close to it lying around.

And the calls kept coming in.

Friends and Enemies

On paper, I was rich. I owned all sorts of properties. But the problem was that I had too many deals and not enough money. I couldn't get the cash together to pay off the people I owed. And I owed a lot of people.

I had always figured that if something like this happened, I could just refinance the properties to get the cash I needed. But after Lehman Brothers, refinancing became a lot harder. I may have borrowed a million dollars on a building a few years ago, but now I couldn't get anywhere near that.

Some of my friends had given me their life savings. They trusted me with everything because I told them it was a guaranteed success. Now that they'd lost everything, they were depending on me, and I just didn't have it. And they were getting impatient.

Soon, it was more than just phone calls. One day, I went out to my car, and my tires had been slashed. The next night, I was sitting at home, and I heard a CRASH! Somebody threw a rock through my window and then sped away. The message was clear: "Give us our money."

I was afraid if it went on much longer, it would just keep escalating. Today it's a slashed tire and a rock through the window. Tomorrow, maybe they'll do something to hurt me or my family. I had to do something.

It's not like I wasn't trying. I was losing everything I had by just trying to pay them back, and it still wasn't enough. I was in so much debt, and I couldn't think of a way to get out of it, except one.

A Way Out

Those two months in 2022 were one of the worst periods in my life, but it wasn't the first time I've dealt with depression. It's something I've had to deal with all of my life, ever since I was a kid in Poland. It also wasn't the first time I'd had thoughts of suicide. The first time those started creeping in was this moment in 2008, as the reality of my position dawned on me.

I hadn't just screwed over my business. I'd screwed over my whole life and the lives of my friends. I couldn't see any other way out except to check out permanently. I had life insurance. That could pay everyone off. My problem would be solved. My family would be safe. And I wouldn't have to look my friends in the eye and tell them I'd failed their trust in me.

So why didn't I do it? Because there was another way out, and eventually, I found it. I solved the problem, and my depression and my suicidal thoughts went away. And the solution came from somewhere I never expected.

A Better Way Out

"Why is Daddy always so upset?" my daughter had asked. I didn't think I could feel any lower, but her innocent concern over my outburst only added to the pain. I didn't hear the response, but I assume it was something like, "Because Daddy needs money."

A minute later, there was a knock at my office door, and my daughter came in.

"Daddy, you need money?" she asked.

"Yes, dear," I said. "Daddy owes a lot of money to a lot of people."

"But you have lots of money!" she said. "We get money out of the apartments all the time!"

The apartment buildings I owned all had coin-operated machines: laundry machines, vending machines, etc. Every two weeks, I would take my two daughters around to the different apartment buildings we owned and collect the money from the machines. They'd put the coins into Ziploc bags, and then we'd take them to the bank. It was my way of teaching them the value of earning and saving money. It was also a good way to spend time with them, and we all looked forward to it.

"Don't worry, daddy," she told me. "We can go to the coin machines and get the money from the other apartment buildings."

My jaw almost dropped to the floor. I couldn't believe it.

I was thinking about killing myself, and my six-year-old daughter had just led me to an idea that could solve my problem. I could get money from the other apartment buildings! No, I couldn't get the $7 million I owed from coin-operated laundry machines ... but there was still money in those buildings I could use.

THINKING OUTSIDE THE BOX

For weeks, I had been looking at the one, big 128-unit apartment building I had all my money locked up in. It was worth $20 million. All I needed was $7 million, but nobody could give me an equity loan that size. The big lenders were all going bankrupt.

But my baby's coin idea opened my eyes. I had money in other places too! To be precise, I owned a lot of smaller units, too, and the small lenders were still doing business.

I took my daughter in my arms and hugged her tight. "I love you," I told her as tears streamed down my face. "You just gave Daddy the answer! Thank you, baby!"

The next day, I started making lists of all the buildings I owned: duplexes, fourplexes, ten-units, twelve-units. Next to each entry, I wrote how much I thought I could get from it. After that, I was on the phone with the banks, talking about refinancing. None of the buildings alone was worth $7 million. But from one duplex, I could get $50,000. From a fourplex, maybe $70,000. From a 10-unit, $200,000. And so on. Soon, I got enough money together, and I paid off everybody in just 40 days.

For weeks, I'd shut myself in my office, trying to solve the problem on my own, afraid of what anybody would think of me if they knew I had failed. And then, when I finally opened the door, the solution turned out to be so simple that a six-year-old could see it. Looking back, I can't help but wonder: How much pain could I have saved myself if I'd just asked for help right from the beginning?

But that was a lesson I wouldn't really learn for another few years.

THE GIFT – BEING

30 HOURS IN A HOLDING CELL

When you have a lot of money, you also have a lot of people who want to screw with you. They want a piece of it or just think they deserve what you have more than you do. Whatever the reason, a lot of people don't like you, and if they're in a position to make your life difficult, they will. It can make international travel very difficult. You always have to talk to your lawyers first to make sure you're free to cross borders. Well, one day in early 2024, I wasn't.

I was in Panama for stem cell therapy. It was supposed to be a short trip. But when I tried to return home, Passport Control stopped me.

"Sir, I'm going to need you to come with me."

"What is it?"

"Our records show you had a development dispute with a contractor in the Dominican Republic."

"Yeah, so?"

"And you failed to appear in court."

Uh oh.

"You have an Interpol Red Notice. We have a right to hold you."

Then they led me down a long staircase, through a labyrinth of hallways, past door after door, all exactly the same. At first, there were signs saying, "Baggage Claim this way" and "Passport Control that way." I noticed that every time there was a sign that said "Exit," we went in the opposite direction. Eventually, the signs disappeared, leaving just that long thread of hallways.

Eventually, we got to a big, metal door that opened into an airport holding cell. And that's where they left me. It was just a tiny little room, about 6 feet by 8 feet — the size of a prison cell. The walls were beige, with a few yellowish stains from age. The floor was diarrhea brown and freezing cold. In fact, the entire room was freezing cold, and I didn't have a jacket. There wasn't even a bed (or blankets) — just an uncomfortable plastic chair. And two big guys sitting by the door to make sure I couldn't leave.

They brought me into that room, and they left me there for the next 30 hours.

Sitting and Waiting

An Interpol Red Notice is a notification to law enforcement worldwide to arrest and detain a person pending further action. This whole thing was crazy, though. They took no further action that day.

And they never even brought me before a judge or took me to an actual jail cell or told me what I needed to do to get things resolved. I was ready to pay a fine or do whatever it took to get back on the plane and go home. But they never had me do anything. Never asked me any questions. They just left me in there. For a long time.

When I was finally released, Jessica quickly arranged for a new flight home. My family had been terrified something was going to happen to me. Would it be two days? Three days? And how about after that? Would they let me go home, or would they send me back to the Dominican Republic, where I'd just come from? And if they did that, how long would it take me to get home from the Dominican Republic?

They assumed I'd be furious after the whole ordeal, but when they saw me, I was actually smiling! I was more at peace than they'd seen me in a long time — maybe ever.

"That was the best 30 hours I've ever had," I said to Jessica.

"What's wrong with you?" she asked. "You've just been locked up. How can you be so calm?"

"Babe," I told her, "That's the first time in my life I've ever had 30 hours to myself."

Freedom in Aloneness

For the first hour, I was mad as hell. How could they do this to me? In the second hour, I started to panic. I didn't know how long they were going to keep me there or what they were going to do to me.

But then I realized there was nothing I could do about it. Whatever was going to happen was going to happen, and I just had to wait for it. I let it all go. And it was one of the most freeing things I've ever experienced.

My whole life, I've been driven by work: working to make money, working to prove myself, working to shut out the feeling of Not Enoughness. That's all I did — work — for 51 years. Now, here I was for the first time with no work to do. There was nothing I could do, even if I wanted to. No business to run, no family to spend time with. I'd done what I could to get this charge cleared up and get them to send me home, but that was in my lawyer's hands now and in Jessica's. There was nothing more I could do about it alone in this cell.

Suddenly, I had nothing to do but spend time with myself. And I realized something: With all this work I did, I was completely avoiding working on myself.

I went up to one of the big guys guarding the holding cell.

"I need paper and a pencil," I told him.

"No," he said. "Nothing that could be a weapon."

"Come on," I said. "I'm not going to stab anybody."

So, what did I plan to do with it? I wanted to journal. As soon as I realized what a unique opportunity this was, I wanted badly to write down the experience.

But they wouldn't let me have what I needed, so I started meditating instead.

MEDITATION AND DISTRACTION

I'd tried meditation for years. Raul had given me some meditations when I went to his boot camp. But I was never very good at it. I was always in my own head.

"Clear your mind," they say when teaching meditation.

But how? There are always a thousand different thoughts in my head. What I have to do today, what I did earlier, the conversation I just had, the conversation I don't want to have...

I'd sit there for a few minutes, and all I could think about was all the work I could be accomplishing. If I meditated on anything, it was the idea that this whole thing was wrong, and then I'd give up and get back to whatever it was I was doing.

All the work I did though paid off in the jail cell.

In the holding cell, there wasn't anything else. All I could do was just sit there and listen to my thoughts. It's amazing what happens when all stimuli are taken away, and you're sitting alone on a plastic chair in a cold, blank room with just yourself. None of the distractions were there. None of the hiding places. It was just me. Interpol wasn't asking me any questions, but I interrogated myself until I broke.

Before this, the closest I'd gotten to that experience was when I was doing the Ironman races. My head was never so clear as after a race. My body was physically exhausted, but my brain was free to daydream, to process things, to have ideas. But still, it was only for a short time.

But here in the holding cell, I was able to have that clarity, that mental freeness, for the next 28 hours. So, who the hell am I without the distractions and the hiding places? I started breaking down my personality — all my different personalities, all the different parts that make up who I am. A businessman, an athlete, a warrior, a king, a husband, a father. A person with depression. A person with an addiction.

With all that stripped away, who am I?

WHO AM I?

After 30 hours in that cell, I came out knowing who I was — and it's who I still am. *I'm the witness.*

I'm the one who sees all those things: all the different things I am and all the different things I will be or could be throughout my life. I serve those personalities as best I can, both the good and the bad. And I make sure I'm protected no matter what happens.

Sometimes, that "protection" takes the form of addiction to alcohol or any one of a hundred other toxic behaviors. They were defense mechanisms to deal with whatever was happening in my life. And then, as they became bigger problems, I needed new personalities, new protections against those toxic parts of me. But in the end, they're **all parts of me**. Both the good and the bad have made me who I am.

MEDITATION ON MY OWN TERMS

Ever since that day in the holding cell, I meditate every day — to get rid of the distractions, forget about everything else, and just take the time to listen to myself. To witness who and what I am. Of course, the time duration now is about 20 minutes, not 30 hours, but it's on my own terms, and it's helped me in so many ways.

Peeling back those layers takes time, effort, and a lot of work. That's why I was never really able to do it before. So often, working on myself was something I avoided. But when I finally did it, I discovered it was essential to my growth as a human being.

It's not easy, but it needs to be done in any way you can. Stop and listen to yourself, and understand where you are, what you are, and who you are. There's incredible freedom in the process, and there's no substitute for it — not even the mental clarity of physical exhaustion that comes after an Ironman competition.

The sooner you can start on that process, the better. You can do like I did and wait for the opportunity to come to you, but not everyone is so lucky as to spend 30 hours in a holding cell in Panama. You're much better off starting the work on your own before it comes to that. The journey won't be easy. But the destination is worth it.

THE CURSE – FEELING ALONE

ON TOP OF THE WORLD

After I finally paid off my debts from the crash of 2008, I started making money again. A lot of money. I was back on track, and things were going according to plan. So much so that, in 2010, I decided to retire early. I'd spent 15 years buying properties and paying mortgages, and I was done.

I'd "retired" before, but I still couldn't help but keep working: a sale here, a business deal there, still always busy with the company I was supposed to have given up. This time, I went completely hands-off. I stepped away and let the business run itself while I focused on other things.

What sort of other things? That was just it: I didn't know.

I'd spent my whole life working to achieve my goals: a successful business, multi-millions of dollars, every luxury I could imagine... I'd finally gotten it all. I had nothing else to do. Nothing else to look forward to. And I was still young! I had my whole life ahead of me, but what did I want to do with it? What was a challenge worthy of someone so driven?

All my life, I'd been addicted to the pursuit of something, and I still needed something to pursue.

Walking away from the Olympics had been a nagging regret, and now, with all this free time, the idea of competing in sports was alluring. I decided to try the Ironman competition, a triathlon kicked into overdrive. The Ironman is a 2.4-mile swim, followed by a 112-mile bike race, and then finished off with a grueling 26.2-mile marathon. It's one of the most difficult athletic challenges in the world. And I was going to conquer it.

When I first started, the goal was just to finish it. But then it turned out I was really good at it. So, I started competing in more of them. I was training four hours a day and traveling around the world to pursue my latest addiction. And the more I did, the better I got. Soon, I wasn't just finishing. I was winning.

Triathlons became to me what business had been just a few years before. It was like a drug. I threw everything into it. It made me feel invincible.

ANOTHER KIND OF CRASH

And then one day, it all came crashing down. I was on a skiing trip, and I had an accident. A bad one.

Suddenly, there were no more marathons, no more bike races. The doctors weren't even sure I would come out of it with both legs. I spent six months in and out of the hospital, dealing with infection and all sorts of other problems. I looked like hell. I lost so much weight that people thought I was dying.

And the depression set in again. That feeling of Not Enoughness. Losing my strength meant again losing my purpose.

Before I retired in 2010, I had defined myself as a businessman. Without that, what was I? So, I became an athlete. That was my life. It was who I was. Now that I couldn't do that anymore, what could I do? What was I?

It wasn't just not being able to compete anymore. How could I be a father to my children if I couldn't run with them, play with them, and be active with them?

And once again, the suicidal thoughts started.

I was all alone again, in my head 24/7, and the demons were after me. Every day, they kept telling me I wasn't good enough. And here I had totally messed up my life again with a stupid skiing accident. That's what happens to losers, I thought.

Being alone with myself back then wasn't a good thing at all. I felt truly cursed.

Road to Recovery

With antibiotics and 13 surgeries and six months in and out of hospitals, they were able to save my leg. Slowly, gradually, I recovered. In fact, rehabilitation became my pursuit — my newest addiction. And as I focused on it, the depression left, too. Just as it had with my debt, the depression went away when my problem was solved. But it was a sign that there were deeper problems going on. Any time things started to get tough, I would mentally break down.

And nobody knew it but me. I put on my poker face and acted like everything was fine so nobody knew anything was wrong. And because I forced myself to go through all of this alone, there was nobody to help me.

What would I even have said to people? "Poor me. I never have to work again. My kids and grandkids will never have to work. I've achieved everything I ever set out to do. I'm so miserable."

But that was part of the problem. Since I'd already reached all my goals and I didn't have to work anymore, I felt like I was useless. My kids were provided for. I wasn't contributing anything to society anymore... So, what was I still living for? Once my recovery was complete and the depression left me alone, I decided I needed to figure that out.

THE IMPORTANCE OF A STORY

I started looking at life coaches, motivational speakers, and self-help gurus. I started with Tony Robbins. I went to his seminars. Then, I went to any other seminar I could find. I'd go through their programs, I'd read their books, I'd watch their videos.

I still remember watching self-help videos on Facebook at 2 a.m., when I heard a man tell his story.

"I was successful. I accomplished everything," he said. "And then I lost everything, and the depression set in."

That was me!

He went on. He told about how he had immigrated to the U.S. from Ecuador. How when he was just a kid, he started hustling to earn extra money, selling everything from used video games to T-shirts to the other kids in his neighborhood at a hefty markup. How that eventually led him to become a real estate tycoon, and how, after losing it all during the 2008 housing crash, he found a way to use the disaster to his advantage and become more successful than ever.

And then he talked about his family, how the emotional traumas from when he was a kid carried over into his adult life and drove him to drink the pain away until he could barely function anymore.

His story was so close to what I had gone through myself. I didn't know it at the time, but I was listening to the man who would become my friend, my mentor, my life coach, and the person who, 12 years later, I would be lying to on the phone every week, telling him I was OK. That was the first time I encountered Raul.

What I did know was that I **had** to talk to this guy as soon as possible. I applied to his program that night. The next morning, I got a call.

"Tell me your story."

"Who are you?" It wasn't Raul. "I want to talk to Raul," I told him.

"You can't talk to Raul," he said. "You have to talk to me first. Once I preapprove you, you can talk to Raul."

This guy I don't know wants me to just start telling him all about my depression and my thoughts of suicide?

"Screw that," I said. "I don't want to go through some middleman. I want to talk to Raul."

"If you're not ready to tell me your story," he said, "Then don't waste my time."

Who did this guy think he was? Did he have any idea who *I* was? Nobody talks to me like that. I thought about hanging up right then and there. But I didn't. Now, he had my attention. And now, even more, I had to know who this guy was who would make me jump through all of these hoops just to talk to him.

"I gotta know your story, bro," the guy said. "Are you ready to change your life?"

"I'm ready for anything," I told him. And then I told him my story. At the end of the call, he scheduled a call for me with Raul.

DECIDING TO GO TO THE NEXT LEVEL

A few days later, Raul called me and hit me with the same line. "Are you ready to change your life? Are you ready to go to the next level?"

"I don't know what I want," I said. "I just know I don't want to feel what I'm feeling. I want someone to take me out of this place."

Then we talked — for a long time. And by the end of the conversation, I was signing up for his program. I didn't even know how much it cost, but I knew whatever the amount, it was worth it.

Three days later, I was in New York for Raul's boot camp. It was intense. It was unlike anything I'd ever been through. But it was amazing. And it was the first step toward getting me out of that dark place and helping me get my purpose back. The journey was far from over, and as you already know, there were still plenty of dark spots to come. But that was the beginning.

And it all started with my reaching out and asking for help.

WHAT'S YOUR REASON FOR LIVING?

As men, especially, we're taught to put walls up. We're taught not to need anybody. If you can't do everything by yourself, then you're useless. If you show your emotions, you're weak. We're not taught to ask for help or to do the deep, inner work on ourselves. Anything that's not on the surface gets bottled up, hidden away, and ignored.

AS MEN, ESPECIALLY, WE'RE TAUGHT TO PUT WALLS UP. WE'RE TAUGHT NOT TO NEED ANYBODY.

I learned from years of painful experience that that kind of toxic masculinity will kill you. You can solve the surface problems, and doing that is a quick fix. But if you don't learn how to do the real, inner work, then the real, inner problems will just keep eating away at you. You need to look below the surface and really explore who you are and why. What are you doing in life? What's your reason to go on living? Figuring that out is the only way to get through whatever crazy stuff life throws at you, both inside and outside.

EVERYTHING IS TEMPORARY

WINNING THE LOTTERY

When I talk about my journey and my success, I like to say that I won the lottery. The truth is, I worked my tail off every day for what I have. What some people call lucky breaks were actually a matter of making the best of whatever situation I was in — including some really bad ones.

But when it came to getting to the United States, I really did win the lottery.

Living in America had been my dream since I was eight years old. "Someday, I'm going to America," I'd tell my father. "I'm going to wear a suit to work. I'm going to get rich, and then I'll retire."

However, getting out of Poland isn't as easy as just deciding you want out. In order to get a green card from the Polish government, there's a literal lottery, and some people wait years, even decades, for their name to be pulled. Year after year, I'd tell my cousins and classmates, "This is the year I'm going to America!" and then my name wouldn't be drawn, and I'd have to wait for another year and another chance at a new life.

I knew people who took the easy way: they'd go on a tourist visa and just stay — illegally. I didn't want to do it that way, so I went through all the right channels, did everything the right way. And in 1993, just days before my 21st birthday, I finally won the green card lottery.

I said goodbye to my family and my old life and boarded the plane to leave Poland.

WELCOME TO AMERICA

Arriving in the U.S. felt like something out of a Hollywood movie. I left a poor, communist country that was shrouded in gray and gloom. And as the plane was coming into America, I saw the New York City skyline for the first time: the bright lights, the buildings — it was incredible! It was like the whole city was alive, and it made me feel alive, too, in a way I'd never felt before.

After I landed, it took eight hours of customs paperwork to get my green card. But those eight hours went by like a minute. I was in heaven. I had to pinch myself to be sure I wasn't dreaming. I was finally in America. It was pure ecstasy.

My godfather had been in America for a few years already, and he'd arranged for me to stay with him when I arrived. After eight hours in the airport, we drove another six hours to his home in Rochester, New York. When we finally got there, it was 2 a.m. It was dark, and I was tired, but even then, I was in awe of his house. Was that a pool? I was living in a house with a pool! Are you kidding me?!

Thrown in the Deep End

There was no adjustment period, no easing into the new situation. At 7 a.m. the following day, my godfather woke me up.

"I need you to cut the grass before you go to school," he said, sounding more like my father than I'd imagined he would.

By 8 a.m., I was in class: English as a Second Language. When class was over, I started my new job: working in a restaurant, washing dishes. You might think that being thrown into my routine so quickly would make the ecstasy fade. It didn't. That feeling of joy and amazement at everything lasted two years. I didn't mind the work. I was used to working hard. Now that I was finally in America, it didn't even feel like work.

In Poland, life was rough. Here in America, people were friendly. It seemed like everyone wanted to help me. I'd be in the back of the restaurant washing dishes, and my coworkers would come up to me and teach me new words. It was amazing!

Breaking through the Language Barrier

The only real hassle I dealt with was the fact that I barely spoke English. I was the same age as my cousins who

I lived with, but they'd been here longer, and they were much more fluent than I was. That made things difficult, but we were making it work.

My aunt was troubled by it, though. Worried that I might be a bad influence, she pulled me aside, and I'll never forget her cold words: "You can't talk to them," she said sternly in Polish.

I was confused. These were my first cousins. I'd known them all my life, and now they were my only friends. And now I was being told I couldn't talk to them?

"Why not?" I asked.

"Because they need to be speaking English," she said. "And if you can't speak to them in English, you can't talk to them."

Far from discouraging me, this just made me all the more determined to succeed. Just because I didn't speak English, I was beneath them? I couldn't talk to my own family?

Spite. It really is one of the best motivators.

I had started my English class in April. The class lasted until September, and by that time, I was fluent. Fluent enough to talk to whoever I wanted and fluent enough to start college. And in just three years, I graduated from SUNY Brockport with a degree in business administration and finance and a minor in economics.

YOUR CIRCUMSTANCES WILL CHANGE

Growing up in Poland, it was easy to lose hope. Surrounded by negativity, I could easily assume life would be that way forever. I feared that no matter how hard I worked, no matter how much I did, this would be all I would ever know.

But after I came to America, all that changed. In America, I discovered all situations in life are *temporary*. The notion that things will never change is a lie. And understanding that has kept me going through a lot of dark times.

Psychology studies have found that when most people commit suicide, it's not because they actually want to end their lives. It's because they want to end their circumstances. Those circumstances are so big and overwhelming that they seem like they'll be with you forever. The negative parts of your life are all you can see, and the only way to get rid of them seems to be to end your life. But it's not, because those circumstances won't be here forever.

Likewise, the feeling of Not Enoughness can rise and fall with our circumstances. In Poland, I grew up being told, over and over again, that I was Not Enough. But in America, I saw the endless possibilities and opportunities. It was so much easier to see that I *was* Enough, and that my hard work really did matter.

That's why this lesson is so important. Our situation may seem bleak now, but everything is temporary. No matter how bad our circumstances are, eventually they will end. We can't define ourselves by our past. We can't pin all of our hopes on a single, anticipated outcome, either. We just have to trust the fact that this won't last forever, and then we must make our way through as best we can.

HOPE – ANYTHING IS POSSIBLE

A LIFE-CHANGING CONVERSATION

It's amazing how one conversation can transform your entire life.

In 1996, I had been in the United States for three years and was just wrapping up my final year of college while working 80 hours a week. One of my side hustles was buying old cars and fixing them up to make a couple hundred bucks at a time. I wasn't getting rich, but it was something I could do to make some extra cash.

Then, one day, my girlfriend's uncle came to visit from Colorado.

He told me he owned a four-unit apartment building. He lived in one unit and rented out the other three. And the income from those other three units covered all the expenses: mortgage, utilities, property tax. Basically, he was living for free.

That one conversation opened my eyes to a whole new world. Suddenly, I had a new plan — and a goal. I was preparing to ask my girlfriend to marry me once I graduated. And now, the timing for a wedding couldn't be better.

The Goal on the Refrigerator

"Instead of wedding gifts," I told my girlfriend, "let's ask our friends and family just to give us money."

If we could raise enough, we'd have it made. To buy an apartment complex, we needed $50,000 for a down payment. I wrote a $50,000 check and stuck it to the refrigerator with magnets. That was the goal, right there, where I could always see it.

When my girlfriend saw it, she thought I was a little bit nuts. At that point in our lives, $50,000 might as well have been $500 million. It was a ridiculous thing to even think about. She started hiding the check from me. It was one thing for me to keep it where I could see it — but if someone else were to come in, did we really want a check for $50,000 out in the open like that?

I reminded her that they wouldn't be able to cash it anyway before we reached our goal. She reminded me that having a check I'd written bounce wouldn't be great for us either. Still, I kept putting the check back on the refrigerator. I needed it there to remind me what I was working for and that anything is possible.

ANOTHER NEW WORLD

Between the wedding cash and my work flipping cars, we eventually saved up $50,000 and moved to Denver, Colorado. The shift from Rochester to Denver was almost as dramatic as the shift from Poland to Rochester.

Rochester was a huge improvement over Poland, but in reality, it wasn't much sunnier in New York. Still, I thought people seemed happier. I certainly was. It was only later that I realized I had been living in a bubble. When I moved to Denver, the bubble burst, and my mind was blown. It was sunny and beautiful, the air was clean, the sky was blue, and the people there were truly happier.

For us newlyweds, it was a dream come true.

The Goal in Denver

The day we moved to Denver, I bought the four-unit apartment complex — my first major real estate purchase. I had found the property already and signed the paperwork, but before we could close the deal, my wife and I both needed jobs to show the bank we were capable of repaying the mortgage.

I got a job as a restaurant manager at Sheraton Hotels. I learned the business and worked my way up. After a few months, they promoted me to banquet manager. Not long after that, they made me food and beverage director. I just kept learning, growing, and advancing. I thought I had it made.

At that point, I wasn't looking to get rich through real estate. Buying the apartment was just a stepping stone.

The goal had been to move to Colorado, where there was an opportunity, where property taxes were cheap, and where I could go skiing whenever I wanted. Owning that four-unit apartment building was just something to provide a basic income and cover expenses while I focused on whatever it was that would eventually make me rich. I thought I would find it in the hotel business.

But that wasn't how things turned out.

SMARTER DECISIONS

If I had known that real estate was where my success would be, I might have learned a bit more about it before making that first purchase — and I would have seen how clueless I was. I put $50,000 down to buy that building. I thought that's what it took to buy a four-plex.

A few months later, I knew better. I bought another four-plex — the one next door to mine. And that time, I put $3,000 down. Not long after that, I bought the four-plex on the other side of mine for $5,000 down. Then I sold them all and used the money to buy a twelve-plex. After that, I bought a 17-unit building, and after that, I bought an 18-unit building.

The whole time, I was still working at the hotel — working my tail off, in fact, and bringing in a huge amount of business. The owner of the hotel also owned six others, and he recognized that mine was a cash cow. The problem was, he didn't recognize why. Our egos clashed, and this career that I had thought was my ticket to the big time started to become unbearable.

A New Direction

That's when I realized something. I owned 73 apartment units by then. My passive income from these apartments was so much more than what I was making at the hotel. So, I walked away from my $200,000-a-year job and retired. The money would keep coming in, and I could travel and see the world.

And I did. I traveled. I skied. I did whatever I wanted — for about six months. This was my first of many retirements at the age of 28. And then I realized something else.

I needed more.

I've been working so hard my whole life. Some people look at how hard I've worked and how much I've gotten done and think I must have some superhuman work ethic. But the truth is, that kind of work is all I've ever known. It's how I was raised, growing up in Poland. Eighty-hour work weeks were just what you did. Even before I started working — when I was six years old, I'd have a full day of school, then swim six hours on top of that. There was no trophy for it, and I never thought of it as some huge accomplishment. It was just what you were supposed to do.

Now, I had all the free time in the world. But what was I without the work? What was I without the goal to strive for? What was I supposed to do now?

Fortunately, my wife had the solution. She saw how well I was doing at real estate, just as a side job, a background income. Just think what I could do if I actually made it my main focus. She also saw the one thing that was holding me back: real estate agents. The ones I dealt with were more a hassle than a help. They slowed down the process, made everything more difficult, and took their cut.

So, at my wife's suggestion, I got my agent's license — and then there was no stopping me. By the end of that first year, I had made a million dollars. And the rest is history.

BURN YOUR BOATS

There's an old saying that's been attributed to everyone from Julius Caesar to Cortez. I first heard it from Tony Robbins. "If you want to take the island, burn the boats."

Keeping your boats gives you a way to leave the island at any time. And if things get rough, and you have a fallback plan or a way out, you're going to use it. But if there's no other alternative than to succeed, then you'll keep pushing until you've got what you need.

Sometimes, burning the boats means sticking a $50,000 check on your refrigerator for a daily reminder of what you're working toward. Sometimes, it means quitting your stable but unfulfilling $200,000-a-year hotel job and getting your real estate license instead. Whatever your goal is, you need to go all in. As soon as you start holding something back, "just in case," you make it that much likely that there will be a "just in case."

I said that everything is temporary. That includes winning. And that's the way it's supposed to be. Your goals are meant to be temporary because they're meant to be achieved. We're designed to keep going. Achieve your goal and move on to the next one. Achieve that one, too. It may take time, but as long as you're moving forward, you're on the right track.

FEAR – LOSING IS LEARNING

ONE THING MISSING

When I first started making money from real estate, it looked like I had everything in the world. I had money and success, sure. But there was one thing I was missing. More than anything else, I wanted kids.

My wife and I had talked about it for a long time. She told me she wanted kids too. But she didn't think the timing was right. She wanted kids someday, but we weren't ready yet. At first, it was because we didn't have the money. Then, when we had the money, other issues stopped us.

The problem wasn't that we weren't ready. It's that *she* wasn't ready. And maybe she never would be. But I was ready now. And the more I pushed to have kids, and the more she pushed back, the more I realized our marriage wasn't going to work.

So, what did I do? Did I sit her down to have a frank discussion about both of our wants and needs in this relationship and what kind of future we might or might not have? No. Dummy that I was, I decided the thing to do was to get a mistress.

Looking back now, I'm not sure why I was in such a rush. If I had just waited a couple of more years until she was ready, would that have been a big deal? No. But as many of us can attest, I thought I knew everything when I was younger. And I wanted what I wanted when I wanted it. I was selfish, without a doubt.

I don't even think I knew for sure that I truly wanted a family; maybe it was more the idea of keeping up with what I saw around me and giving in to societal pressures. Most of our friends were having kids, and hey, that's what you did in your late twenties when you were married, right?

I think I also may have thought that my feelings of Not Enoughness would go away if I just had some kids. They would forever change the insecurities I felt inside. So, as fate would have it, I walked away from real love and, as time would tell, started walking down a very slippery slope.

A NICE POLISH CHICK

Like something out of a bad movie, a friend and I set out on a road trip to find a girl. I'd gotten it into my head that we should go to Vegas. But as we drove down I-25, my buddy had a different notion in mind.

We were coming up on I-70, and he gave me a choice. "We can go west on I-70 to Vegas and find you some girl. Or we could go east to Chicago and get you a nice Polish chick."

My friend had judged me right. We went east.

And there, in a club in Chicago, I met the woman who was to become my second wife. She was eight years younger than I was and full of life. And she wanted to have kids right away. We started seeing each other. Before long, she was pregnant, and I filed for divorce.

I liked her, she liked me, and I saw something special in her. I never dreamed that two decades later, we would be living a very different reality. But I was living in the moment and was very spontaneous and, yes, selfish.

And her liking me also filled up that insecurity that I had felt all my life. Hey, if a really hot girl thought I was the bomb, then I must be, right? She gave me a huge ego boost, and I thought she was the answer to what I needed. I never thought about how it would affect my first wife.

The Moral Hangover

When I finally told my wife I wanted a divorce, she was devastated.

I can't even tell you how guilty I felt after that. Not only was I cheating on my wife, I caused her lots of pain and disappointment. It was like I'd been drunk on bad decisions, and now came the moral hangover.

I gave my first wife everything in the divorce. I didn't even try to fight. I gave her much more than she asked for and more than anyone thought was right or fair, even if I was a cheating bastard. Even the judge tried to stop me.

"You can't just give her everything you own," the judge cautioned.

"I don't need it," I replied. "I'm young, I'm smart, I'm good at business. I can always make more money. But this is my only chance to try to make up for what I did to her."

Of course, being naïve and emotionally immature like I was, I thought that would actually make up for everything or repair the damage that I caused. In the end, it didn't really mean that much. But the way I saw it, I could just use my assets and "buy" the changes that I wanted to see.

"I have to give you *something* in the asset division," the judge said. In the end, I kept one 16-unit building. I let my wife have the rest. And then I went off to marry my mistress.

I still deeply regret how much I screwed up. The whole thing — the divorce and its aftermath — seriously changed the trajectory of my life. Ah, if only we could change the mistakes we made in the past. All we can do is accept them and let them go.

EMBRACING FAILURE

Like I've said, when all is said and done, everything is temporary. The bad times are temporary. But the good times are temporary, too.

You may be on top of the world, but you can't keep winning forever. Eventually, you'll fail. Eventually, you'll mess up so badly that it will feel like the end of the world. And that's one of the best things that can happen to you. Losing is learning.

Fear of failure is one of the main things that holds people back. But without failure, you can't learn. You can't grow. I've enjoyed some amazing success in my life, but I've also had plenty of epic failures — my first marriage and how I handled ending it being one of the biggest. But those failures are a part of who I am. My failures and the lessons I learned from them are what got me to where I am now.

So don't give up just because you screwed up. Learn from it and grow. It is one of the hardest things we'll ever have to do, but it's the journey that's important, not the destination. It's the wisdom you gain that you can only really gain from going through it, surviving, and seeing it for what it is.

You are not your failures. You can let your failures define you and let the fear of failure hold you back and keep you from going after your goals. Or you can own up to them, learn from them, and move on. Make the lesson, and not the failure itself, a part of you.

MAKE THE LESSON, AND NOT THE FAILURE ITSELF, A PART OF YOU.

Embracing your failures makes you stronger. It's the best way to grow. And it's the only way to succeed.

This book is a testament to my failures. It's my way of embracing them and sharing them with you. It's also a testament to my successes. But just as I did, you will learn way more from the mistakes I made and the stories I tell about them than the great successes I had.

THERE'S ALWAYS A WAY OUT

BEATING THE WEAKNESS OUT OF ME

One of the most toxic things we're taught as men is that asking for help makes us weak. We're told that we should be able to handle everything life throws at us, and if we can't, then we're Not Enough. There are so many times in my life where, if I had just asked for help, I could have gotten through life so much more easily.

A big part of asking for help is learning to trust people — learning to be vulnerable with people. In particular, learning to be vulnerable with other men. This has been one of the hardest lessons for me. It's difficult to show vulnerability when you spend your whole childhood hearing that it's a type of weakness.

If I was weak in front of my father, he'd challenge me mentally and emotionally. If I was weak in front of my swimming coach, same thing. If I was weak in front of my teachers, same thing — a hostile environment. After a while, it became ingrained. If my friends were weak in front of me, I sometimes would behave the same way toward them.

That's how it was. When you're weak, you get challenged by it, and the next time, you won't be weak — or you won't *appear* to be weak anymore, which in toxic masculinity is the same thing. Pretty soon, you never show anyone your weaknesses again. On the outside, you're strong and confident. And on the inside, you're always about ten seconds away from a full breakdown.

GETTING WHAT I NEEDED

It wasn't until I met Raul that I learned to be vulnerable. And even then, it was a slow process. Raul had his hands full helping me figure myself out. I remember one morning, I had an 8 a.m. video call with him. A check-in so he could see where I was and how I was doing. Well, that particular morning, I was doing awful. I'd been out drinking until 5 a.m. I knew I had the 8 a.m. call with Raul, and I'd pushed myself to the limit anyway — and well past it.

I looked like hell. I felt like hell. My head was throbbing. I had vomited earlier and probably would again. Raul could tell I was in bad shape. So, what did he, as my life coach, tell me to do?

"Crack a beer," he said.

"What?" I asked.

"It'll level you out and get you on your feet so you can face the rest of the day," he told me.

So, I did that, and pretty soon, I was ready to finish the meeting and face the rest of the day.

A few years later, after I had finally quit drinking, I confronted Raul about that morning.

"What the heck, man?" I asked him. "Why would you tell me something like that? You're supposed to be my life coach!"

"It's what you needed at the time," he said. "I could have told you to quit drinking. But you never would have listened. You weren't ready to hear it. So, I gave you what you needed to get you through the day, until you could get to the point where you WERE ready."

Learning to Trust

He was right. If Raul had lectured me on how alcohol was ruining my life, I would have just resented him for it. But by helping me in the moment, he allowed us to build trust, which would get me to the point where I was finally ready to do what I needed to do: to be vulnerable and to ask for help.

That building of trust allowed me to build trust with other men as well. Gradually, I was able to have a group of guys around me who I could really be vulnerable with and who I could ask for help when I needed it. And having those connections to rely on gave me the strength to pull away from the toxic connections with my family — the ones that made me feel like I was Not Enough.

I had a new group now. It was comprised of people who could see me at my most vulnerable and still think I was Enough — and who would help me through whatever I was dealing with instead of trying to beat the weakness out of me.

THERE'S ALWAYS A SOLUTION

I've talked about how, in some of the darkest times in my life, what finally pulled me out was just getting a solution to my problem. When you're in that low place, it can feel like it's going to last forever. Our brains are wired to remember the bad times and the bad feelings much more clearly than the good times and the good feelings.[1] It's how we learn to avoid danger instead of barreling headfirst into the same bad decisions over and over again.

Unfortunately, it can be a more serious problem when it comes to depression. When you get into a bad place, that's all you can see. It can cloud your judgment and make you think it's always been that way — or that it always will be that way. That's the kind of thinking that leads to suicidal thoughts and self-destructive tendencies.

But there's always a way out. Whatever your problem is, there's a solution. Whatever you're dealing with, there's a solution. And once you come out the other side, you'll see that things weren't as desperate as they seemed. There's always hope.

But in order to come out the other side, you need people around you who you can trust and be vulnerable with.

---

1   Allie Caren, "Why We Often Remember the Bad Better Than the Good," The *Washington Post*, November 1, 2018, https://www.washingtonpost.com/science/2018/11/01/why-we-often-remember-bad-better-than-good/.

When your judgment is clouded by depression and desperation, you need someone else there who can be the voice of reason — even if all you're ready to hear from that voice is, "Crack a beer."

YOU NEED TO LET GO OF HAVING ALL THE ANSWERS YOURSELF.

You need to let go of having all the answers yourself. You need to let go of always having to be strong. There is always a way out. But often, the only way you'll get there is *together*.

WE DIG OUR WAY IN

EVERYTHING I WANTED

Remember, as soon as my first divorce went through, I married my mistress, who was already pregnant with our first child. After our daughter was born, we had two more daughters and a son. Finally, my life had the one thing I had been missing. Everything would be great from here on out. I could be happy. Right?

It wasn't, and I wasn't, though it took me a long time to realize why. My second marriage was a mirror of my parent's marriage. It wasn't a healthy relationship. I didn't know how to honor her, and she didn't know how to do that for me either. The insults would fly daily. I can't speak to how she felt, but I constantly felt like I wasn't enough. I was angry all the time, and so was she. And in my mind, that was normal.

Even though my first marriage had been much more peaceful, it had still failed, so I couldn't use it as a gauge. I thought marriage was supposed to be hard.

I felt terrible about myself and my life. I was Not Enough of a man for her or my first wife.

But since that was how I'd been made to feel my whole life, I didn't realize how toxic it was or how low I was really getting. This was all just what life and marriage were supposed to be about.

A Revelation

And then came my skiing accident. It came completely out of the blue. One moment, I was an Ironman, a champion. The next moment, I couldn't even walk. Six months in and out of the hospital, on the slow road to recovery, not knowing if I'd be able to keep my leg.

I needed a lot of care. I couldn't clean myself properly, but I wasn't a great patient, either. The nurses had to pick their battles. They took care of the wounds, but it was on me to take care of myself, and I couldn't do it alone.

It became clear very quickly that whatever help I needed, I wasn't going to get from my wife. I needed her to help me clean myself while I was lying in bed. She wouldn't do it. She said it was gross. I needed someone to stay with me, do things for me, and even just talk to me for a while.

That was when I finally realized that this wasn't normal. This isn't what a marriage is supposed to be. If she couldn't be there for me when I needed her most, then what are we even doing together? As soon as I got out of the hospital, I realized something wasn't right in our relationship.

The divorce came four years later. Of course, divorce is a lot different when you have kids. As toxic as our relationship was when we were together, being apart was worse for the kids. Our kids lived with her, which means they usually heard her side of the story. I didn't stand a chance. I became the enemy. Not only was I Not Enough for her. Now, my own children believed I was Not Enough as a man or father.

I loved my children. I'd wanted them so badly I cheated on my first wife to have them. And now I was losing them too.

Wow. Karma is a real thing.

YOU ARE NOT THE VICTIM

So, "Poor Jarek, in a loveless marriage at a disadvantage with his own children struggling to find the encouragement and acknowledgement that he desired."

Except, no.

For a long time, I tried to play the victim, but as with most things, there was more to it than that. It's true;, my second wife hadn't been there for me when I needed her. But all throughout our marriage, I was never really there for her, either.

I supported her financially. I gave her material things. But I was never really there. At first, I was working. Then after I retired and became an athlete, I was training. There was always something else taking up my time, keeping me away from my wife. And from my kids.

I almost never saw my kids, even when we were married, and after we divorced, I saw them even less. I had ruined my first marriage for the chance to have children, and now that I had them, I didn't even see them.

That was the lesson that I had to learn. I wasn't a victim, much as I wanted to be. My wife had treated me badly, but it was my own mistakes that had led me to this point. My mistakes had caused me to fail in my first two marriages and to fail my children.

Everything around you is a direct result of your actions. True, sometimes life throws you curveballs, but how you deal with those curveballs is entirely on you. If you want to learn and grow, you can't sit around playing the victim. You need to own every decision and every mistake.

And you need to understand that it's OK that you make mistakes. You still need to take responsibility for them and own the consequences, but you shouldn't be afraid to admit you've failed. There's no shame in admitting that you're still learning. And just because you don't have everything figured out yet, it never means that you are Not Enough.

I know that now.

WE CLIMB OUR WAY OUT

LIVING LIKE A DISHWASHER

When I first met Jessica in May of 2020, I was still figuring out who I was and who I wanted to be. To some degree, I still am, and I probably always will be. But at that time, I was nowhere near the answers. I was pretty lost.

I had more money than I would ever be able to spend in my lifetime. The questions swirled in my mind. Who was I in relation to that wealth? How would that money define me?

When I first got successful, it was about making the money rather than spending it. It was about proving that I could do it and trying to feel like I was Enough. I didn't care about what the money meant beyond that.

Most of what I made went back into making more: another four units, another 16 units, another 80 units.

Meanwhile, even after I made my first million, I was still living the way I had when I was washing dishes. My bills and the mortgage were covered by the rent coming in. Beyond that, I was spending maybe $600 a month. Part of me still felt like just being here in America was a luxury. I didn't need anything fancy.

Eventually, I did start to spend some money. I traveled. I built a huge house with my second wife — the same house that I would eventually spend two months shut up in, avoiding my friends and thinking about killing myself before Jessica got me out.

But even when I did find ways to spend my money, I felt a bit lost. I had enough money to do literally anything I wanted. So, what did I want? What did that kind of life even look like?

LIFESTYLES OF THE RICH AND DECADENT

My friend Jeff knew exactly what that kind of life looked like. He was everything you ever picture when you think of extreme wealth. Every extravagant possession, every decadent vice, every image of rock stars and movie stars doing things you've only dreamed of... that was Jeff's life.

I looked at Jeff and saw everything you see on television and in the movies depicting what a wealthy and extravagant lifestyle is supposed to look like. It looked amazing. And I could afford to live that life too, if I wanted. So maybe I should give it a try.

Jeff had a huge yacht in Miami, on which he would throw parties on the level of *The Great Gatsby* or *The Wolf of Wall*

Street. He'd sail out to sea on this boat full of alcohol, drugs, and beautiful women, and they'd party till dawn.

One day, Jeff invited me to one of these epic boat parties. I had to see for myself what this lifestyle was like. It looked like everything. I had to see if it was me.

Getting on the Boat

I'd only known Jessica for a short time, but I could already tell that she could be a powerful force in my life if I was open to it. A powerful force for what? I wasn't sure yet. As I said, I was still figuring out who and what I wanted to be.

Still, when I got the invitation from Jeff, she was the first person I called.

"I'm going on Jeff's boat," I told her.

"You're not going to like it," she said.

I laughed. Not like it? What's not to like? This was the sort of chance that you don't pass up. I went on the boat.

There were four of us: Jeff, two of his other buddies, and me — plus twenty gorgeous women. The boat was full of willing young ladies void of inhibition and standards. The man-to-woman ratio was staggeringly convenient for men.

Plus, there were bottles and bottles of top-shelf alcohol. Who could ever ask for more?

A few hours after we set sail, I was completely plastered. I looked around at the women, the drugs, the alcohol. What the hell was I doing? I was miserable. I didn't want any of this. There was only one thing I did want. I went into the bathroom and called Jessica.

"You need to come pick me up," I said.

"You're drunk," she replied.

"I still need you to pick me up," I told her.

"How am I supposed to do that?" she asked. "You're miles from shore by now."

"I don't care," I said. "I just need you to come pick me up." Then I went to Jeff.

"Turn the boat around," I told him. "I want to go home."

"Are you nuts?" he asked. "The party's just getting started! I'm not going to turn it around!"

"Fine," I said. I gathered up my wallet, my phone, and my keys and headed for the edge of the deck.

"What the hell are you doing?" Jeff asked me.

"I'm going to swim it," I said. It wasn't that far. Maybe 20 or 30 miles. I was sure I could do it.

"Screw you," Jeff told me. He turned the boat around.

I finally knew what I wanted. And it wasn't on this boat. Instead, she was waiting to pick me up when I got off. Jessica and I went home, and I never went near Jeff's boat or Jeff's lifestyle again.

It was a big wake-up call. And divine intervention, I'm sure.

MAKING BETTER DECISIONS

As I said, many of the things that went wrong in my life were the result of my own bad decisions. So, the only way to craft a better life moving forward was to make better decisions.

If you own your mistakes, you learn from them, and you grow. And then you take a better path.

A big part of that is choosing who you keep around you. Who are the people you let into your life? Because those people will influence who you are and how you act. Really know them, who they are, and what impact they have on your life. And then choose the ones who will make you better.

A few years before, I would have chosen to stay with Jeff and the beautiful women on the boat. I would have kept partying and drinking and reveling in the decadence, and I probably would have destroyed myself. But that night, I chose Jessica instead, and I'm grateful every day that I did.

Once again, you need to be willing to ask for help. It's one of the most difficult things you can do, but it's necessary. You can't do life alone. We all get ourselves into difficult, dangerous, or just plain stupid situations. And if you can't bite the bullet and turn to those people in your life that you can count on — the Jessicas, the Rauls — you'll never be able to get out. The people who weren't afraid to tell me the truth about myself and the situation were so important — a complete departure from the "yes men" who were along for the fun ride regardless of the consequences.

It can be a long, slow journey. But the only way to do it is step by step. Move forward. Make a bad decision. Ask for help. Make a better decision. Move forward again. Repeat, for the rest of your life. And bring the people around you with you. Be there for them, just as they are for you. We're all in this together, struggling to figure out how to get through life — and the only way to do it is with each other's help.

WE'RE ALL IN THIS TOGETHER, STRUGGLING TO FIGURE OUT HOW TO GET THROUGH LIFE – AND THE ONLY WAY TO DO IT IS WITH EACH OTHER'S HELP.

GOOD DECISIONS COME FROM THE HEART AND SOUL

BRONCOS FAN FOR LIFE

Ever since I first moved to Colorado, I've been a big football fan. From the first time I watched one of their games on TV, they were my team. And I've followed them ever since. I watch every game, and I go see them play whenever I can. Like Jack Nicholson with the L.A. Lakers, that's me with the Denver Broncos. I would die for the Broncos.

So, you can imagine my excitement whenever they had a big game.

Every Saturday night, I would go with my friend to a high-end restaurant in downtown Denver. It's a great place with amazing food, and it's where all the celebrities go. If you want to get up close and personal with the rich and famous in Denver, you go there.

Meeting Your Heroes

Well, we were at the restaurant the night before a big game, eating, drinking, having fun, when who should walk in but three of the Broncos' star players! Like I said, this was a hotspot for celebrity sightings, but still, it was really exciting! These guys were my heroes.

They walked into the restaurant and headed straight for the bar, where they proceeded to order shots of whiskey.

"They're doing shots the night before the game?" my friend said to me in disbelief.

"It's just one shot," I said. "They're probably just trying to relax a little before tomorrow."

A few minutes later, though, they ordered another round of shots. And another. Then, the shots became full glasses. And they just kept knocking them back.

And it's not like I was watching them closely to analyze their every move. Of course, they caught my attention when they came in because I'm such a fan. But they weren't exactly keeping a low profile, either. And the more they drank, the louder and rowdier they got. They were pretty hard to miss — as these men — my heroes — proceeded to get pretty drunk.

Disaster and Disappointment

So, how did the big game go? How do you think it went?

Three of our star players were barely able to stand upright, much less play football. They stumbled through the game, making every mistake, missing every opportunity. The sportscasters wondered what could be wrong and said they must be having an "off day." I wonder what they would have said if they'd seen these players in the bar the night before.

The Broncos lost. Badly.

And it was totally preventable. If they'd just saved the drinking and partying for after the game instead of before, they could have won. Or if not, at least they could have given it a good fight and lost with a bit of dignity. But instead, they threw it all away. They changed the trajectory of the rest of the season, and they let us all down.

FEEDING THE EGO

What did I learn from all of this?

For one thing, never meet your heroes. They'll never measure up to the picture you've built up of them in your mind. They'll end up disappointing you.

But that wasn't my main takeaway. The lesson I learned was about the decisions we make and the people they affect. I don't know what was going through the heads of those Broncos players. Did they not care whether or not they won the game? They're making millions either way. Or maybe they thought so much of themselves and their abilities that they figured they could go into the game hungover and still beat their opponent.

Whatever they were thinking, it came from a place of ego. They weren't thinking of their fans, who were counting on them. They were only thinking of themselves.

Now, I'm hardly one to judge someone else for bad decisions made with alcohol. I've made plenty of them myself. I've disappointed people who were counting on me, both drunk and sober, and I've got two failed marriages to show for it. And just like with my Denver Broncos, my bad decisions were made out of ego.

Letting People Down

When we make those decisions, we're thinking to ourselves, "I want a drink," or, "I want to stay up all night partying." We're not considering the ramifications. We're not considering how those decisions will impact the people who might be counting on us.

Those Broncos players had all sorts of people counting on them. Their teammates, for one. The ones who DIDN'T go out drinking the night before the big game... who made sure they were healthy and well-rested and prepared to give it their best. They had to carry those three players who showed up hungover and couldn't pull their weight.

And, of course, those three players let their fans down, too. Millions of us were watching the game, counting on our Broncos, cheering for them. If those players had taken the time to consider all of these ramifications, maybe the men would have thought twice before drinking the night before a big game.

A HIGHER STANDARD

Now, in fairness, these players were a bunch of kids at the time, not more than a few years out of college. We all make dumb mistakes at that age. Not to mention, with their talent and success, they'd been praised and fawned over for years. That kind of treatment can get in your head. It feeds the ego and makes you think you can do no wrong.

I can relate. My success fed my ego too, and a lot of the mistakes I made came from that ego. But whether you like it or not, when you're in a position of power or prestige or success, you need to hold yourself to a higher standard.

That includes me, too. My wealth and success mean I have influence over people. People look up to me. People count on me. And when I make bad decisions, I let those people down. Or worse yet, I set a bad example for them that they'll then follow into their own bad decisions. It's something I need to keep in mind when considering the ramifications of my actions and on whom. Those effects can go a lot farther than you realize.

GOD, THE DEVIL, AND YOU

In the first chapter, I talked about the devil who whispers in your ear, telling you you're Not Enough.

But that's not all he says. Sure, when you're down and insecure, he'll tell you you're Not Enough. But when you're on top of the world, he'll feed your ego. He'll set you up with distractions and temptations. And the more you listen, the more he'll talk.

He'll tell you things like, "Why don't you party the night before a big game?" or, "Why don't you drive to Chicago and find yourself a mistress?" He'll make you think you deserve things that are bad for you, that you're entitled to anything and everything you want.

And then, when it all blows up in your face, that's when he'll start telling you again that you're Not Enough.

So, how do you get rid of the voice of the devil?

First, you have to stay connected to God. Now, that means different things to different people. I'm not here to start a theological debate. But what I mean is, **stay connected to something greater than yourself** — whatever that means to you. Something you can rely on to keep your ego in check and remind you that there IS something greater than yourself. Something worth being better for and worth holding yourself to that higher standard for.

And second, you need to stay connected to your purpose. Whatever the devil is telling you, it's a distraction. It's something that will tear your focus away from what really matters. And the farther away you fall, the less in touch you become with who you are and what you're supposed to be doing. In my opinion, the devil feeds the worst parts of your thoughts and can hinder you from living authentically to be the person you truly can be. Furthermore, the negative thoughts can cloud the goodness of your heart and soul.

Staying connected to God and to your purpose will give you something else to listen to when the voice of the devil starts taking over. It will help you to drown out that voice with something stronger, more positive, and more powerful that will keep you focused. And that, in turn, will lead to better decisions, made not from a place of ego but from the soul.

DAMAGING DECISIONS

WHAT I'D ALWAYS WANTED

I mentioned earlier about how I've always wanted kids. My whole life, I wanted to be a father. I ruined my first marriage because I wanted kids. I jumped immediately into a new relationship because I wanted kids. So, once I finally had kids, you'd think I'd be a good father, right? That I'd want to bond with them, spend time with them, and be a dad to them. Well, it didn't work out that way.

I have four kids: three girls and one boy. And for a long time, I had zero relationship with any of them.

I could blame it on my ex-wife. When we got divorced, she was the one taking care of them, and because I wasn't around, they believed the worst about me. But the truth is, I wasn't around for my kids long before we split up.

Driven by Work

From the time I was a kid, I was driven by work. That's what I did with my life, remember? I collected glass bottles. I did odd jobs. Then I came to this country, and I washed dishes while going to school. Then I was in hotels. Then, real estate. I worked 80-hour weeks as a matter of course. Everything I did, every job I had, I poured myself into, body, mind, and soul.

Sounds like a great work ethic, right? Only, the 80-hour work weeks didn't leave me much time to spend with my children. Every two weeks, I made the time to take them around to the buildings I owned, collect the change from the laundry machines, and take it to the bank. That was the time we spent together. Other than that, most of the time I worked.

Chasing the Ironman

And then I retired. Stepped away and let the business run itself. So then I finally had as much time as I wanted to spend with my kids, right? Wrong.

That was when I started training for the Ironman. All I had ended up doing was trading one obsessive pursuit for another. Though I wasn't spending all day in the office anymore, now instead, I was spending all that time either training or recovering from training. And I still wasn't spending any time with my kids.

"Daddy, come play with us!"

"I just did a hundred miles on my bike. I'm tired."

"Daddy, come to the movies with us!"

"I can't. I'm getting a massage."

"Daddy, come lie on the couch and watch TV with us!"

"I need some time to myself."

I could say that my ex-wife turned my kids against me, but in many ways, I myself turned them against me. I was always a good provider to my family. I gave them everything they needed. Even during the crash, when I was millions of dollars in debt, I made sure that my kids were taken care of.

But I didn't build a relationship with them. What they really needed was me: my presence, my encouragement, my emotional support. And that's the one thing I didn't give them.

I've come a long way in the last few years and done a lot of work on myself. And now, finally, I'm at the point where I really do want a real relationship with my kids. But, because of my past mistakes, building those relationships has been an uphill battle every step of the way.

WHEN GOOD DECISIONS GO BAD

It doesn't take some great enlightenment to know that binge drinking the night before a big game is a bad decision. I'm sure even the Broncos players didn't think it was a GOOD decision. But their egos got in the way, so either they didn't care about the consequences or thought they were above them. Either way, objectively bad decisions tend to be easy to recognize, so long as you keep your ego in check. What's a lot harder to spot are the good decisions that can end up turning into bad decisions if you're not careful.

Training for Ironman competitions was, on the surface, a good decision. It's healthy and stimulating, and it helped give me purpose when I was lacking it. What I didn't realize is that I was only continuing the cycle I'd experienced in my childhood.

The reason I pushed myself so hard was because my coaches, teachers, priests, and parents made me feel like I was Not Enough. I had to prove myself by working harder, doing more, going further. So I did. But in doing so, I neglected the people I love. And that made them feel like they were Not Enough. They wanted my attention, but I was too busy for them. I wasn't there for them, and I didn't build a relationship with them. I didn't realize for a long time that I was making them feel like they were Not Enough for me.

Every Decision Has Consequences

This brings us right back to what I just talked about in relation to the Broncos players: considering the ramifications of your decisions and how they might affect the people around you.

The difference in this case is that *I thought I was trying to do the right thing.* But there was still collateral damage. I still hurt the people I cared about, leading to another failed marriage and the loss of my kids' trust and respect. My supposedly good decision spiraled into a series of bad consequences and broken relationships.

The problem was that even though I was trying to make better decisions, that desire was still coming from a place of brokenness and pain. I hadn't started healing yet. And when your soul is hurting, you do things that hurt others, even when you don't mean to.

My decisions were still coming from that place of Not Enoughness that had driven me to succeed in business and then, after I retired, to prove myself as an Ironman athlete.

I told myself I was training not just for myself but for my family too. Because, what would they think of me if I didn't have a goal to strive for, a purpose to live up to? They'd think I was Not Enough.

But that decision was coming from my ego instead of from my soul. And because of that, in order to try to be my idea of what would be Enough for them, I neglected to give them *what they really needed* — myself. That would have been Enough for them. And it's what I'm trying to give them now.

I understand now that the consequences of my actions may be different from what I intend. Even when I'm trying to make the right decisions, I can still end up doing the wrong thing. I'm not perfect, and I never will be. The healing is ongoing.

But part of the healing process is about recognizing when you've made those decisions with your ego instead of your soul. Once you've done that, you can understand and own up to the consequences and try to make amends as best you can. Learning from your mistakes is the only way to move forward and make better decisions in the future.

HEALING DECISIONS

TOP OF THE MOUNTAIN

When it comes to healing and making better decisions, my time spent with Raul as my life coach and my membership in his program have helped me in more ways than I can count — in more ways than I probably even realize. The work we've done has been an important part of my healing process. But when it comes to the progress I've made, I always have to remember not to get too cocky. The process is ongoing. I am healing. I'm not *healed*. I will never be fully healed.

It's dangerous to start thinking that you're "healed" or "recovered" or that the progress you've made is permanent. That's when those "good decisions" made from ego start to take over. But the consequences can be even more severe than that. Because as soon as you start thinking you've got it all figured out, that's when the storm is about to hit. And it's when you're on top of the mountain that you're most in danger of falling all the way down it again.

Shut Down

I first joined Raul's program in March of 2018. It's a year-long subscription, so every year around mid-March, I renew my membership. This means that in 2020, I was renewing my membership right as the pandemic hit, and the whole world went crazy.

Depression soared during the pandemic. The isolation, the uncertainty, the constant onslaught of disease and death — these were hard on all of us.

Up until that point, I'd been doing really well for quite a while. I was healing; I was making progress. I thought I had everything figured out. I was on top of the mountain. And then everything started to crumble.

It's amazing what a few months of isolation will do to you. All the work you've done and the years of progress you've made can slip away in just a short time. Suddenly, you find yourself dealing with thoughts and emotions that you thought you were rid of for good.

I went into a downward spiral. I hated myself, and I hated these circumstances that I had no control over. What was the point of even getting up in the morning in a world that looked like this?

This feeling is not at all unique. The pandemic and the global shutdown hit a lot of us in the same way. It came like a bolt out of the blue and upended every-thing — everything we had, everything we were doing, everything we were looking forward to. Suddenly, overnight, the world looked completely different, and we had to find ways to adapt. The irony is that we were all going through the same things, but we were all going through them *alone.*

The shutdown was supposed to be just two weeks. That's what they told us. Two weeks at home, and we could stop the spread of COVID and let the disease die out. After that, we could all go back to our regular lives, happy, healthy, and safe. But then weeks turned into months. "Just hold on a little longer," they told us. "Just a little bit longer, and this will all be over." They kept telling us that — but still, there was no end in sight.

Someone to Turn To

It didn't take weeks or months to break me down, though. The feelings of isolation and uncertainty hit me all at once. I was a mess by the end of March. And this was just before I met Jessica, so I didn't yet have my queen by my side to help me through it as she did a couple of years later when she got me out of my room.

There were a few friends I could trust to help me through the storm. Raul was one of them.

Fortunately, I didn't make the mistake of shutting Raul out and pretending I was fine like I did later on. Our weekly check-ins became daily. We would talk on Zoom, and I would tell him about the hell I was in. And he would help me — or try to. The problem was, he could help me with me, but he couldn't change the state of the world we were living in. It seemed like nobody could. Nobody could even tell us how much longer it was supposed to last. So what was the point of going through this, day after day?

The End

One day, on a call with Raul, I had just had enough, not of Raul, but of the pandemic, of life, of everything. It was too much.

"I just want to tell you goodbye," I said to Raul.

"Great, I'll talk to you tomorrow!" he replied.

"No," I told him. "I won't be here tomorrow. This is goodbye."

"Like hell it is," he said. "You've come too far. You can't quit now."

"Raul, you're a great guy," I told him. "You've helped me through so much. But I think this is beyond any of us. I'm checking out."

I tried to end the call, but he wouldn't let me.

"Don't go anywhere," he said. "Stay with me. You're not getting off this phone." For an hour and a half, he told me that. "You're not getting off this phone." For an hour and a half, he talked me down from the ledge. And then finally…

"Promise me we'll do this again tomorrow."

The thought of tomorrow seemed unbearable.

"Promise me we'll do this again tomorrow," he said again.

Every day was exactly the same, with seemingly no hope.

"Promise me we'll do this again tomorrow."

What was one more day?

"Fine, I'll talk to you tomorrow," I told him.

So, I talked to him again the next day, and we went through the same routine. Me, teetering on the edge, Raul, pulling me back. And again, making me promise to talk to him the next day.

And the next day. And the next day. That's how it went. One day at a time. And slowly but surely, he pulled me back from the ledge.

CONTINUING THE JOURNEY

The decision to keep seeing Raul, to talk to him again the next day and the next instead of giving up, was really a decision to admit that I still wasn't healed. Of course, at that point in my life, I felt about as far from healed as I ever have. But the decision was about admitting that there was more healing still to be done. More healing I COULD do. Which meant there was still hope.

Rather than giving up, I made the decision to continue the journey, to stay on the path that Raul had helped me get on. Rather than running away from the people and relationships in my life that mattered most, I would stay in the fight, and we could get through it together. That time of isolation helped me to understand the value of the connections I had.

Looking Inside

What Raul helped me understand during those dark days of the pandemic was that we're always healing. I thought I had come so far, only to fall again. I was so wrapped up in the progress I had made that when hard times came again, I was completely blindsided. And it almost destroyed me.

Carl Jung said, "Who looks outside, dreams. Who looks inside, awakes." Now, there's nothing wrong with dreams. I've spent my whole life chasing my dreams and achieving them. But that's only part of the picture. While focusing on my dreams, I was always looking on the outside. From qualifying for the Olympics to coming to America to achieving success first in the hotel industry, then in real estate, then as a triathlete, my eye was always on the next goal.

The problem was, when I had my eyes on what I wanted to achieve, I was forgetting to turn them inward. Even when it came to my personal progress with Raul, I was focusing on everything I'd done and how far I'd come. If I'd been looking inside myself, I would have seen much sooner how far I still had to go.

Looking outward is also very much about looking forward. You're looking toward your next goal, your next deal, your next achievement. That was my whole life.

But looking inward is about looking backward. Looking back on the things you've done, the mistakes you've made, the people you've hurt. If you don't look back and learn from those things, you'll just keep making the same mistakes again and again, hurting the people you love in the process.

The only way to heal is to look inward,

> **THE ONLY WAY TO HEAL IS TO LOOK INWARD, TO LOOK BACKWARD AT THE THINGS YOU'VE DONE THROUGH THE LENS OF WHAT YOU KNOW NOW.**

to look backward at the things you've done through the lens of what you know now. That's the only way your vision can become clear. By looking into your own heart, you can understand the decisions you've made and their consequences, both good and bad, intended and unintended. Then, you can use that knowledge to make better decisions. And the healing process continues.

AS THE BODY GETS OLDER, THE SOUL GETS STRONGER

THE "RIGHT" ADDICTIONS

One of the reasons healing has been so difficult for me over the years is that I keep choosing drugs that don't look like drugs. I talked before about how good decisions can turn into bad ones and how healthy behaviors can become unhealthy ones if you let them.

And as I also mentioned, my two major addictions were work and the Ironman races.

When you drink or do drugs, people get concerned about you. They hold interventions to tell you that you're destroying yourself and your relationships. But when the drug that's consuming you is training as a triathlete, nobody says anything about it. No one ever had an intervention to say, "Jarek, we think you're getting too healthy." But that didn't make it any less of a problem.

I'd spent my life pursuing those addictions, first with my business, then with my training — and hell, even my recovery from my accident was just another obsession. I pushed myself to get better and stronger and to start walking again. I sought out the best treatments, the best therapies, the cutting edge of medicine. Every part of me was consumed with the idea of being made whole again.

Invincible

Throughout my life, I had defined myself by what I could do. What my body was capable of reflected who I was as a person.

Whenever I achieved my goals, I proved I was Enough. But whenever I couldn't achieve my goals, I proved I was Not Enough.

When things were going well, I thought I was invincible. Then, when it turned out I wasn't, my whole world came crashing down. But the problem was me.

We, as people, are not invincible — nor should we be. If you're invincible, that means you can't be beaten. That you never fail. And as I've said, if you never fail, you never learn. If you go around thinking you're invincible, then you're never able to grow.

Bodies vs. Souls

Our bodies don't reflect what's inside us. Your physical abilities don't make you a good or bad person. Neither do your physical disabilities. If you suddenly find yourself unable to do the things you could do before — whether because of some accident or misfortune or just through getting older — it doesn't make you any less of a person. It doesn't make you Not Enough.

The body is just a shell. It doesn't carry much weight or meaning. Your body's health or brokenness doesn't have any bearing on who you are as a person — on the state of your soul.

No matter how much we take care of them, our bodies age and decay over time. Eventually, our minds start to fail, too. But our souls have the opportunity to grow and get stronger. Our experiences make us better, wiser people — but only if we put in the work.

Like physical healing, emotional healing requires hard work and training, and the results we want can take time to start showing.

And we can't do it without help. With physical healing, we need doctors, physical therapists, and others who understand the problem and know what we need to get better. With emotional healing, we need people who have been where we are, who have experienced these things, and who know what it's like on the other side. They know what we need in order to grow and mature, and they can guide us and help us find the right path. With their help and the right therapies, if we really commit to doing the work, we can come out stronger than ever before.

TEARING DOWN

MEETING JESSICA

I first met Jessica on a dating app. It was May of 2020, just a few months after my breakdown at the beginning of COVID.

I was doing better, but I still had a long way to go. And I still had plenty of self-destructive behaviors that I needed to deal with.

We started chatting, and almost immediately, I asked her if I could call her.

"I don't really do that on here," she told me. "I'd rather keep things on the app."

But I kept asking, and eventually, she gave me her phone number. After all that waiting, the day she finally gave it to me couldn't have been worse timing — I'll tell you why in a minute. But I called her anyway. We talked for a bit. It was amazing. In our first conversation, we connected immediately. We had a great conversation that

I had to cut short as I was literally on my way to a date with another woman. (I didn't tell this to Jessica for years; I told her I had a business meeting.)

Jessica was perfect for me. For one panicked moment, I even worried that she was too good to be true — that maybe she'd been sent by my ex to set me up. But she was all real, and she was amazing.

REALIZING WHO YOU WANT TO BE WITH

I went on the date, but driving over to see her, I kept thinking about Jessica. When I got there, the woman was very nice. We made some polite small talk, but all I could think was that, instead of talking to the woman in front of me, I wanted to be talking to the woman in Miami. I cut things short, and as soon as I got in the car to go home, I called Jessica again.

"That was a short meeting," she said. "It's only been about half an hour since we talked!"

"Yeah, it ended early," I told her. "Do you want to come over?"

"Come over?" she asked. "To Fort Lauderdale?" People in Miami don't like coming to Fort Lauderdale.

"Yes," I said.

"To the house of a guy I barely know?" she asked.

"Not like that," I said. "I'm having some people over for a barbecue. Would love for you to join. There's safety in numbers, right?"

"OK, she said. "But just so you know, as soon as I get to your place, I'm dropping a location pin and sharing it with all my friends so they know where I am and that I'm safe."

"That's fair," I replied. "You won't regret it."

So, we hung out that night. I was actually a nervous wreck the whole night, trying to make a good impression. But apparently, I did because two days later, she agreed to come and hang out on my boat with me. And then, a day or two after that, we got together again. Since it was during COVID, there was nothing else to do, so we just kept hanging out.

I've said before that it took me a while to get my act together during that time and figure out who I was and who I wanted to be. It was six months before we became exclusive. At any other time, that wouldn't be that long, but in 2020, it was an eternity.

WHAT PARTNERS DO

One of the reasons I was reluctant to commit, even though I knew I was with the right woman, was because of my past experiences. Between the relationships in my family that I'd grown up seeing and the two marriages I'd been in, I had an idea of what relationships were supposed to be like — and it wasn't something I was anxious to do again. But Jessica opened my eyes to a type of relationship I'd never experienced and made me realize what I'd been missing.

One morning, a friend and I were supposed to go to Jacksonville. It's 350 miles from Miami, so we had to start out early. I had set my phone alarm for 4 a.m. and put it on vibrate so I could get up without waking Jessica. I got out of bed and was tiptoeing around the room to get dressed and ready when suddenly...

BEEP! BEEP! BEEP!

How did that happen? I swore I turned off the sound on my alarm! But when I checked my phone, I realized it wasn't my alarm. It was Jessica's.

"Morning!" she told me sleepily.

"Babe, what are you doing up?" I asked.

"I wanted to see you off!" she said. "Hang on, I'll go make coffee."

I was blown away. Both of my ex-wives would have stayed asleep. And if I'd woken them up accidentally, I'd never hear the end of it. But not only was Jessica happy to wake up early and see me off, she didn't even think it was a big deal.

"This is just what partners do!" she told me.

Covering For Me

That became a common phrase in our relationship. I'd be completely blown away by some act of selflessness she was doing for me, or I'd see her bend over backward to help me out or make me more comfortable. And she never thought it was a big deal. I'd try to thank her, and she'd wave it off. "That's what partners do."

Then there were bigger gestures, too. One evening, we had a few people over to the house. Nothing fancy, just a few close friends and my kids. And I was drunk. I was drunk before the guests even arrived. Once they did arrive, I probably would have kept drinking the rest of the night. But Jessica stepped in.

She helped me into the bedroom and closed the door. When the guests came, she told them I was a little under the weather and was resting. She kept them company for a few hours and sent them on their way, as they asked her to pass on their wishes that I feel better. Then she came back into the bedroom to get me.

"Why did you do that?" I asked.

"Did you really want them to see you in this state?" she asked. "There's no way you were getting through tonight without doing or saying something you'd regret in front of the people you care about."

"I know," I told her. "Thank you. All I meant was, why would you go to all this trouble to cover for me like this?"

"That's what partners do," she said.

In the world I was from, that was not what partners did. Some people would have paraded me in front of everyone. And they would have kept bringing it up for years afterward.

This is what I was used to in relationships. This is what I had seen my whole life. This is what I thought partners did. But Jessica showed me something different.

HOW YOU DESERVE TO BE TREATED

We expect from people the treatment we think we deserve. When you feel like you're Not Enough, you expect to be treated like Not Enough. It becomes a vicious cycle. You expect to be treated like you're Not Enough, and so you surround yourself with people who treat you like you're Not Enough. And as long as those people treat you like you're Not Enough, you keep assuming that that's the way you deserve to be treated.

Then once you believe it, you start repeating it to yourself and to others, which just makes it seem even more true.

Part of my healing has been trying to build a better relationship with my kids. It hasn't been easy. I've made mistakes, and even on the road to improvement, I continue to make mistakes. I'm only human, after all. Because I've made those mistakes, it's difficult for my kids to trust me, and when my kids don't trust me, it's easy for me to think that I've failed as a father.

For a while, whenever I would talk about my kids and how strained our relationship was, I'd add, "I'm the worst dad ever." Eventually, it became almost mechanical. Any conversation about my kids, I'd say, "I'm the worst dad ever."

Then, one day, Jessica asked me, "Why do you keep saying that? You're not the worst dad by a longshot."

"Yes, I am," I said. "They're the ones who said it, not me. They keep telling me how bad of a father I am."

"Why don't you ask them why?" she said.

Ask them why? I hadn't thought of that. Why would I? The fact that I was a terrible father just seemed obvious to me. Look at all I had done—and hadn't done.

Still, asking couldn't hurt, right? So the next time my kids told me I was the worst dad ever, I replied, "Why? What makes me the worst dad?"

"Because you don't make breakfast for us," was their response.

I was floored. It wasn't that I mistreated them or wasn't there for them. It wasn't that I had failed to take care of them. The terrible parenting that I constantly berated myself for was that I didn't make breakfast for my kids in the mornings.

THE VOICE

If you listen to the devil's voice long enough, he doesn't have to whisper in your ear anymore. Eventually, you start doing the work for him. I've spent years saying terrible things about myself: bad father, bad husband, bad friend, bad person. The worse I feel, the more I say it; the more I say it, the more I believe it, and the more I believe it, the worse I feel.

Then, when anyone else says anything bad about me, I just take that as confirmation. But what they think when they say it and what I hear may be two different things. I may think I'm the world's worst father, who has failed his kids on a fundamental level. But really, I'm just a dad who didn't make breakfast this morning. A dad who supports his kids, who loves his kids, who makes mistakes, but who wants to do right by them.

To keep yourself from getting stuck in your own head, it's important to try to see yourself from the outside. Look at not just what people say about you but how they see you. It can be difficult, especially when you already have your own set view of who you are. But there are two ways you can do it.

The first is just to ask. Be aware of the language people are using and ask them what they mean by it instead of just taking it as it's given. What people mean when they say negative things about you and what you hear are likely to be two different things. People throw words around without thinking about them. Do they really mean what you think they mean?

And the second way is to find people who can show you how things are supposed to be — who can show you what partners do. Or what friends do. People who can give you that outside perspective and let you know that things can be better. That things are supposed to be better.

Finding and surrounding yourself with those people is how you deal with the devil's voice — with your own voice — telling you that you're Not Enough. Find people who can show you that there's a better way. That what you've experienced all your life isn't the norm. With their help, you can finally break the cycle. And then, you can be that friend, that partner, that person to those around you as well.

BUILDING UP

EVERYTHING BUT PURPOSE

By the time I was 34 years old, I had everything I ever wanted out of life: money, success, a wife, kids, the whole package. And I was miserable. You know the old expression, "What do you get for the man who has everything?" Well, when you ARE the man who has everything, what do you get for yourself? What do you DO with yourself?

I'd done everything I wanted. I'd retired, and the business was running itself. So, what was my purpose? My wife and kids were provided for, and as I said before, I wasn't really spending much time with them. I could have just disappeared one day, and no one would feel my absence. I didn't need anything, and nobody needed me. So what was I supposed to do?

I've talked before about how, when I felt a loss of purpose after retiring from my business, I turned to Ironman competitions. Training became my new, all-consuming purpose. Then, when the accident took that away, recovery became my purpose. But after I was recovered, what then? No need to work. Healthy and in good shape, but no longer able to compete. No need to keep working out. Nothing to prove to anyone anymore. What was I supposed to do?

No Questions

So, I went looking for my purpose. But how do you do that? Where do you start? I didn't know where to go to find answers. Worse than that, I didn't even know what questions to ask.

When I first started swimming, I had swimming coaches to teach me. Before I became a success in business, I studied business administration and economics. When I was in recovery, the doctors gave me treatments, therapies, and exercises to do. In working toward each goal in my life, I had knowledgeable and experienced people to guide me, to show me the way.

But what if, instead, my swim coach had just said, "Let me know if you have any questions about your training, and I'll answer them, and that's how you'll learn to swim." Or if my doctors had said, "Do you have any questions about your recovery?" without actually discussing my options with me?

Without having started on the process yet, I'd have had no frame of reference. How would I know what to ask? That's what it was like when I was searching for my purpose. Without anyone to guide me through, how could I know to ask the questions that would lead me to the answers I wanted?

No Answers

That was where Raul came in. When I first started talking to him, he asked me a lot of those questions.

"Why are you here?"

"I'm miserable."

"Why are you miserable?"

"I don't know. I just don't like who I am."

"What don't you like about it?"

"I don't know. It doesn't feel good."

"Why not?"

"I just feel like I don't belong here."

He kept asking me questions. "Is this the problem?" No. "Is that the problem?" No. I knew what the problem wasn't. I just couldn't pin down what it was. So, my answers were mostly just, "I don't know," and "That's not it." I sounded like a dummy. Fortunately, that was just the beginning of the process.

BOOT CAMP

I'd checked out plenty of motivational speakers, self-help gurus, and life coaches before Raul. They have seminars. Raul has a boot camp. At that boot camp, I met a lot of people just like me who were looking for answers but didn't have the understanding to ask the questions. Under Raul's guidance, we were able to give a name to what was missing from our lives and then begin searching for it.

On the third day of Raul's boot camp, he brought us to a cemetery.

"Go and find a headstone," he told us. "Find it, look at it, sit with it. Pretend that it's yours."

So, I found one. And I started imagining my funeral. Who would come to it? I thought hard. I couldn't think of anyone. Was I a good enough husband to either of my ex-wives that they would want to come to mourn me? Was I a good enough father to any of my kids that they would care when I was gone?

What about my friends? Sure, I had them. I hoped they would come. But who? Who did I even really talk to enough for them to consider me a friend? What if the people I knew couldn't be bothered? What if the people I cared about most couldn't clear their schedules for one afternoon to pay their respects to me after I die?

And then I thought about the gravestone itself. A whole life, boiled down to a sentence or two. What would it say if it were mine? I thought about it for a long time.

"Here Lies Jarek. He Had Money."

What else was anyone going to remember me for? What else had I done with my life?

I completely broke down. I started yelling at the gravestone.

"Money!" I yelled. "What the heck good is money?! I made money! It screwed me!"

ISOLATION

I realized that money was one of the things that was keeping me isolated. I had worked so hard to make it. Now I was constantly worried that anyone who tried to talk to me or to be nice to me was really just trying to screw me over and get my money.

And so, I didn't talk to anybody. But since I didn't talk to anybody, I didn't have anybody to share my life with. If I had a victory, there was nobody to celebrate with me. If I had a failure, there was nobody to commiserate with me. I was spending my life alone. And if I kept on that path, I would die alone.

The day after boot camp was over, I went to Starbucks, like I do most mornings. When I got to the front of the line, the barista greeted me—one of those casual, customer service greetings.

"Hi, how's your day going?"

"Pretty well, actually," I said. "I just had an amazing experience the past few days. I really think it's changed me for the better."

"I can tell!" he told me.

"Really?" I asked. "How?"

"Because in all the time you've been coming here, this is the longest we've ever talked," he said. "And I think it's the first time I've seen you smiling."

He was right. I had been so closed off from interacting with anybody that even at Starbucks, I'd pretend to be on my phone so I wouldn't have to make small talk or interact any further than giving my order.

"To be honest," he told me, "Seeing you drive here every day in your Rolls Royce and then not talk to anyone, we just thought you were some rich jerk."

"I was," I said. "But I'm trying not to be."

ROADBLOCKS

Not everyone was so happy with my transformation. When I told my second wife about it, she laughed.

"I just want to be more open," I told her. "I want to be able to talk to people and share my life with them."

"And who's going to listen?" she asked. "Who's going to care about what you have to say?"

This knocked the wind out of my sails a bit, I'll admit. As you start getting well, some people start trying to tear you down. But it was a genuine fear of mine. What if there wasn't anybody who would let me open up to them? What if all anyone cared about was what I could do for them?

But I didn't let my fears stop me. I kept doing the work to become a better, more open person who could connect with the people around him. It didn't happen overnight, of course. It took Raul years to break down my walls. And like I've said, healing is not healed. I still have work to do, and I always will. But the lessons I took away from that boot camp have helped to drive me ever since.

LEARNING FROM EXPERIENCE

The problem with achieving success so young is that it had warped my view of reality. To combat my feelings of Not Enoughness, I had set out to prove that I could do anything, be anything, have everything. And when I did, it made me think I was untouchable — that I could do no wrong.

So then, when I did fail? It had to be someone else's fault. It couldn't be me. I'd trusted the wrong person. I'd let the wrong person in. And that was why things were going wrong. So, the solution was to stop letting people in.

One of the things that Raul drilled into me over the course of years is that failure is a part of life. And sometimes it IS my fault. But that we learn from experience. The older we get, the more we experience, including both successes and failures. And we learn from both.

But it's essential to your spiritual health to share those experiences with others, both good and bad. The only way to understand them is through the lens of the people around us. Without those people, we get trapped in our own bubble, isolated. And when we're isolated, we keep making the same mistakes over and over again.

I thought for years that the walls I put up made me stronger. But the only way to grow and learn is to tear down those walls. Sharing our experiences with others helps us to build relationships, and it's through those relationships that we grow stronger.

Sharing our challenges allows other people to help us shoulder the load. Sharing our successes gives us people to celebrate with, which gives meaning to what we've done. Sharing our fears gives us people to support us, comfort us, and get us through. Sharing our hopes gives us people to encourage us, to root for us as we pursue those hopes.

SHARING OUR EXPERIENCES WITH OTHERS HELPS US TO BUILD RELATIONSHIPS, AND IT'S THROUGH THOSE RELATIONSHIPS THAT WE GROW STRONGER.

By sharing with others and letting others share with us, we grow stronger together. Finding people we care about, working together with them, and being there for each other is what makes life worth living. And if you're trying to find something to give your life purpose, other people are the best place to start.

THE EVOLUTION OF THE SELF

THE NEVER-ENDING ROAD

When people talk about "the road to recovery," it makes it seem like recovery is a destination you can get to. Just follow these steps for this amount of time, and you'll reach Recovery. But as I've said, the process is ongoing. You're never fully healed, but you are always healing. You never stop doing the work.

This was important for me to learn as I recovered from my depression in 2022. For weeks, I was in bed; I couldn't leave the room. Then, finally, I got out of the house.

I thought at first that it would be as simple as just having a crisis and getting through it. I'm used to getting results immediately. That's how I'm designed. I set a goal for myself, I put everything I have into it, I make progress, and ultimately, I achieve it. So, that was my approach to getting through my depression.

But it doesn't work like that. The process was slow as hell. When Jessica got me out of the room, that was the turning point, but it wasn't the end. I still had a long way to go. And it was far from a smooth road.

Getting Out

One thing I had to do was get active again. During those eight weeks, I wasn't training, I wasn't exercising, I wasn't really moving very much at all. And because exercise gives you endorphins, lack of training creates a vicious cycle. You feel depressed, so you don't exercise, but because you're not exercising, you continue to feel depressed. Once I finally got outside again, I knew I was going to have to break the cycle.

Swimming has always been my main activity. Even now that I do the Ironman, every three to six months, I'll do a round of water feats. I'll spend a week and a half doing nothing but swimming and water exercise, pushing myself as far as I can. But after my breakdown, I just didn't want to do it. The thought of getting in the water was more than I could handle.

But I pushed through, and I tried it anyway. I got in the water and started swimming. I made it about half a day into my 10-day regime before giving up. I couldn't bear the thought of doing this for a week and a half.

FAILED EXPECTATIONS

After my swimming failure, I decided to focus on biking instead. In Ironman competitions, I would bike for 100 miles, then run a marathon afterward. I'd done long-distance biking plenty of times. It should be a breeze, right? I set myself a goal of doing a two-hour bike ride.

But I couldn't do it. As soon as I got on the bike, the thought of doing this for two whole hours just made me depressed. Even just that little bit felt like a mountain I couldn't scale.

And then the devil's voice started whispering again, and the feelings of Not Enoughness resurfaced.

"Look at you. You promised yourself you'd do two hours. You promised yourself you'd get active. And now you can't even do it. You pushed yourself to recover from your skiing accident, and now, even though you're in fine physical condition, you can't even push yourself to do a simple bike ride. What good are you? You're a failure. You might as well just go back to your room and crawl into bed."

There was no way I was going back into my room. Not after all I'd done and all Jessica had done to get me out of it. I had to figure something out.

MAKING REALISTIC PROMISES

When it came to training and physical activity, I was used to giving it 200 percent. If I did anything less, I was conditioned to see it as a failure.

But not being as physically active as I had been wasn't my only problem. I realized that by making these promises to myself and not keeping them, I was fueling my depression. Those broken promises made me feel like I was Not Enough.

If I was going to get past this, I couldn't break any more promises to myself. I realized my physical training expectations weren't realistic. You can't expect to instantly go from 0 to 200. You're just setting yourself up for failure.

I'd already been working on baby steps to get me out of the house. Get out of bed. Go to the living room. Take a walk around the house. Go out the front door. Go to the end of the driveway. I needed to do the same thing with physical exercise. My promises to myself needed to be tiny.

With that in mind, I changed how I talked to myself and how I set my goals. I didn't say, "My goal is to bike a hundred miles," or "My goal is to bike for two hours." I'd just say, "My goal today is to ride my bike." Or, "My goal is to take a walk." Even if it was just 500 meters around the block, the goal wasn't distance. The goal was just to get out of the house and do something.

I'd go out and do a little two-mile loop around the neighborhood. I didn't tell anybody about it; I just went. I didn't want to hear anybody saying, "Two miles? That's it?" I know, logically, that my friends wouldn't have said that to me. Jessica certainly wouldn't have. Raul wouldn't have. They'd have been proud of the progress I was making. But I didn't want to give my inner voice a chance to tell me that's what they were thinking.

EVERY LITTLE STEP FORWARD

Every time I got out of the house and got on my bike or went for a walk, it was a humongous win for me.

Keeping the goals small and simple was what allowed me to start doing more. If I had said, "I'm going to bike for two hours every day," even if I made it the first day, and the second, maybe the third day I'm not up to it, and I only do half an hour. I've failed my goal, so the next day, I don't go at all, and I have to start over from square one.

Setting the goal of just doing it helped me keep going even on days when I wasn't feeling it. On those days, I could do more if I wanted to, but I didn't have to. The main point was that I was doing it vs. not doing it. Any movement forward was better than staying still. I'd been staying still for eight weeks, and I couldn't go back to that.

By setting those tiny, attainable goals and by keeping those little, bearable promises to myself, I slowly started building up resilience.

That resilience helped pull me out of my depression and get back to my life, and the buildup of my physical strength helped me build up my mental strength, too. I started making small, manageable promises to myself in other areas.

"I'm going to respond to my text messages today instead of letting them sit unanswered for days." Responding the same day became responding within an hour. Then the promise became, "I'm going to call and text the people I care about first instead of waiting for them to get in touch with me."

Building up my physical resilience again took two or three months. Building up my mental and emotional health again took two years. And it's still an ongoing process.

HEALING THROUGH VULNERABILITY

As I write this, I'm at the point where I can do Ironman competitions again. I can function normally in my life and do the things I was able to do before my depression without struggle.

But I'm not the same person I was before those eight weeks in my room, and I never will be again. Nor should I be. We're designed to reinvent ourselves, to recreate the idea of who we are and who we should be, over and over. Whether we realize it or not, we're here for the evolution of our souls.

Sometimes, that evolution happens because of external circumstances. We take what life throws at us, and we deal with it. Things like two months in the house during a pandemic, crippled by depression. Things like six months in and out of the hospital after a skiing accident. Adapting to these circumstances and overcoming them changes us. Hopefully, it will change us for the better — but that's up to us.

The key is to allow yourself to be vulnerable. If you're the sort of person who never bends, eventually you'll break. But if you embrace vulnerability and believe that you don't have to be strong all the time, then you can find the strength you need. By recognizing that what you *can* do is Enough, over time, you'll be able to do more.

EMBRACING THE CRASH

It's also important to find meaning in the crashes. There will always be crashes. There will always be setbacks. You may not know when, but you can still be prepared. Brace yourself for those crashes and lean into them. They're part of your journey. You need to fail in order to learn. You need to crash in order to build yourself back up. If you understand that, you can come out the other side, not fully healed, but better, stronger, and wiser than you were before. Just remember, it can only happen one step at a time.

The phrase, "Today is the first day of the rest of your life," is somewhat of a cliché, and its meaning isn't always clear. But here's what it means to me. Today is a new beginning. Whatever happened yesterday doesn't matter. If you failed yesterday, today you have another opportunity to get it right. If you didn't meet your goal yesterday, today you can make a new goal. If you broke your promise to yourself yesterday, today you can try a different promise. Just wipe the slate clean and start again. Yesterday isn't what's going to take you into tomorrow. Today is going to do that.

Today is the first day of the rest of your life. So how will you spend it?

THE OLD YOU

"NEVER AGAIN"

I was 14 years old the first time I tried alcohol. This was back in Poland on an overnight class trip. That evening, someone brought out a bottle of vodka, and we started passing it around.

Since I'd never drunk before, I hadn't built up a tolerance yet, and I ended up much drunker, much sooner than I had anticipated. Soon, the room began to spin like a helicopter. I was dizzy. Feeling like I was going to throw up any minute, I went to my teacher.

"I think there's something wrong," I told her. "My head is spinning. I've got a splitting headache. I need you to take me to the hospital."

"You don't need a hospital," she told me. "You're just drunk."

She took care of me, and after a lot of vomiting and a killer hangover the next morning, I was fine. But it was such a miserable experience that I vowed never to drink again.

I realize that that's become a bit of a cliché. It's what everyone says after a bad night of drinking. But in my case, I actually didn't drink for a long time afterward. Whenever I thought of alcohol, all I could think of was the vomiting, the headache, and the helicopter spinning. Why would anyone want to do that to themselves? I certainly didn't.

AND BACK AGAIN

I didn't drink again until I was 30, on the night I drove to Chicago to find a mistress.

What made me start drinking that night? Well, we were in a club. Alcohol was literally all around. Everybody else was drinking. And I knew that if I wanted to mingle and meet people, being the only non-drinker in the club wasn't the way to do it. So, I had a Corona.

Imagine if the only time you'd ever been in the water, you were wearing weights on both ankles. You flail around, you struggle just to keep your head above water, and you nearly drown. So you vow never to attempt to swim again, and anytime you even think of the water, you think of that time you nearly drowned.

Then years later, when you finally go into the water again, it's in the Great Salt Lake. Not only do you not have the weights on, but you're so much lighter than the salty water that you find you're able to stay afloat without even trying.

That's what the difference was like between drinking vodka in Poland and drinking Corona in Chicago. The

Corona was only 4.5 percent alcohol. I felt nothing, which meant I could have another one. And another one.

And gradually, I built myself up to drinking more and more. Now that I no longer saw alcohol as a looming pillar of death, I was free to enjoy it. And enjoy it. And enjoy it.

WHY "NEVER AGAIN" NEVER WORKED

I did know how to stop — or at least how to pause. I was able to take a break from drinking a few times. When I started training for Ironman, I didn't drink for two years. Another time, a friend and I went to Mexico and drank for seven days straight. When it was over, I had a moment like the one in Poland. I had a hangover that made me feel like I was going to die, and afterward, I couldn't even look at or think about alcohol. I stopped drinking for another two years.

I also stopped drinking right after I filed for divorce from my second wife. It was a lot to deal with, and I wanted to make sure I was completely clear. And the last thing I needed was for my ex to bring evidence into court of me being a drunk. So, I got things under control and kept myself sober through the whole process.

Then, on July 7, 2020, my divorce was finalized. And that's when I got stupid.

I remember making myself a drink to celebrate. I didn't have to be on high alert anymore! I could just enjoy myself! So, I made up for lost time. I was drinking more and more, getting completely plastered and making a fool of myself. Fortunately, I had Jessica to hide me away when things got really bad. I don't know what I would have done without her, but I probably would have alienated a lot of my friends.

Then I went to Europe. I was gone for two months, and I realized I was drinking every single day. But did it really matter? I was on vacation!

When I got back, I'd go back to my healthy lifestyle: eating right, working out, staying sober. That's what I told myself, anyway.

I came back on a Friday. That night, I had a few friends over to play poker, and I got drunk again. And again, Saturday and Sunday. I had meant to work out Monday, but I was too hungover to do it.

The hangovers were part of my self-destruction. The physical pain was awful, but it wasn't just that. When I was hungover, I would break promises to myself. Those broken promises sent me into a downward spiral of self-loathing. And to dull the pain of the downward spiral of self-loathing, I would drink again.

At first, even when I was getting drunk, I was only drinking with other people. I drank to be social, to have fun, to connect with people. That was why I started drinking in the first place — to connect with people at the club. I still went overboard sometimes, but at least my friends were there, going overboard with me.

But during that period after my divorce, that's when I started drinking alone. It wasn't social, and I wasn't connecting with anyone. I was just sedating myself. I would drink until I passed out. It wasn't fun anymore. It just became what I did.

Seeing the Pattern

When I looked at my drinking patterns over the course of my life, I realized something. Whenever I wasn't drinking, I was successful. It was before I started drinking that I made my fortune in real estate and retired at 28. When I stopped drinking to train, I won triathlon competitions.

But whenever I started drinking again, those were stagnant parts of my life. When I went to Raul because I lacked purpose, it was when I was drinking. Was I drinking because I was unfulfilled? Or was I unfulfilled because I was drinking?

At that point, I hadn't made the connections yet: the hangovers leading to the broken promises, the broken promises reinforcing my ongoing sense of Not Enoughness, or my drinking contributing to my lack of purpose. Some of these thoughts had come to me before, but I would always dismiss them and just have another drink.

What I did realize each time was that alcohol was keeping me from the things I wanted to be doing, that I should be doing. So, I would put drinking on hold again for a little while. But then, slowly but surely, I would start up again: a drink one night, two drinks the next, and so on.

The Devil You Know

Alcohol had become my security blanket. When things were difficult or stressful, I went back to drinking. When things were better and I felt a sense of relief, I went back to drinking. And whenever I felt like I was Not Enough, alcohol would shove those feelings into the background and keep me sedated.

They say, "Better the devil you know than the devil you don't." Alcohol was a devil I knew intimately. It had its consequences — the awful hangovers — but I knew those too. And dealing with the splitting headaches, the vomiting, and the feeling like absolute crap seemed preferable to a life without my security blanket.

Our brains are wired to seek out patterns and cling to them — even ones with negative consequences. They like the familiar, the routine.[2] That's what makes it so easy to fall into addiction. There's comfort in those routines. But that comfort can hold you hostage, and your routines can turn into a slow death.

The more you get used to a thing, the easier it is to keep doing it. The first time I drank, it was something unfamiliar and unpleasant, so my brain rejected it for years afterward. But by starting slowly and building up, I inadvertently ended up establishing patterns, which became harder and harder to break.

But if you're going to grow and evolve, you need to move beyond destructive patterns. Repeating the past isn't evolution. It's de-evolution. Over time, repeating negative patterns again and again degrades you and makes your destruction more and more tolerable.

Of course, not all patterns are harmful. Some of them can be beneficial and even healthy. But if you're going to grow into a newer, better person, you need to take stock of those patterns. You need to look frankly at your past and

---

2   Stacey McLachlan, "The Science of Habit," Healthline, December 22, 2021, https://www.healthline.com/health/the-science-of-habit#1.

understand why you do the things you do. Why did you start doing them? What purpose do they serve? Do they help to build you up, or are they there to sedate you?

That includes the so-called "healthy" habits that nobody raises an eyebrow at. Are you working out all the time because it's healthy, or are you doing it to avoid facing something else? Do you spend all your time in the office because you have a good work ethic, or are you terrified that if you don't succeed, you'll be a failure and a disappointment to the people you love? Who or what are you neglecting when you throw yourself into your patterns and routines?

As you grow and evolve as a person, these patterns become part of your past. A connection to the past is important, but it's up to you to decide which parts of your past you keep and which parts you leave behind. If you're serious about growth and evolution, you may have to discard a lot.

THE NEW YOU

SELF-AWARENESS FROM OUTSIDE

I knew what alcoholism looked like, and I knew how destructive it could be. I'd seen it firsthand. In Poland, drinking was really ingrained in the culture. My grandparents, my uncles, my cousins… It was everywhere except in my house. I don't have any actual memory of the one time my father got drunk. And after that, my parents didn't drink.

But my best friend did. He started drinking long before I did and drank a lot more. Nobody thought anything of it, though. Drinking was what everybody did, after all. As long as he could still do his work and live his life, his wife didn't care, and I didn't care. He was a functioning alcoholic.

And then, one day, he wasn't functioning anymore. He was always drunk, and he couldn't be counted on for anything.

Everybody told me, "Jarek, you have to step up!" So, for years, I helped him, I did things for him, and I saw what drinking was doing to him. I researched alcoholism, hoping I could figure out how to get him clean. I read articles like "The Six Stages of Alcoholism" to get an idea of how bad things were and what could be done.

Learning about alcoholism and seeing what it looks like from the outside made me somewhat self-aware. When I looked at my own drinking, I always told myself that I didn't really have a problem because I wasn't as bad as my friend — that at least I was functioning (even though there were times when I wasn't).

But having read about the stages of alcoholism, the signs, and the behaviors, I started to recognize those things in myself. I could try to deny it all I wanted, but it was evident that I had a problem.

THE FINAL "NEVER AGAIN"

After I got back from Europe in late 2020 and stopped drinking, I thought I meant it, but it didn't last. Slowly but surely, I fell back into my old patterns — one drink followed by two, followed by three, and so on.

And then, in 2021, I went back to Poland for my friend's birthday — back to my hometown, where drinking alcohol was more common than drinking water. We drank for four days straight. I got completely drunk.

At the end of those four days, Jessica flew in to see me. It was February 14, and I wanted to do something romantic with her for Valentine's Day. But I was a complete mess.

I was so hungover I couldn't function. I was in so much pain. And that was it. That's when I told Jessica and then texted Raul and some other friends on the plane home: "I'm done with drinking. Never again."

Accountability

I wasn't stupid, though. I'd said, "Never Again" plenty of times before. I would quit for a week, for two weeks, for a month, and then I'd go right back into it. I'd get into the frame of mind that the problem was only when I got completely drunk. If I could keep it under control, it would be fine. Just one drink wouldn't hurt. But one drink today becomes two tomorrow, and soon, I'd be back to binging.

Therefore, I didn't trust myself. I wanted my decision to stick. I had to make it so one drink WOULD hurt. So, I took extraordinary measures. There's a chemical you can have injected that reacts with alcohol in your body and makes you sick. It's a slow-release injection and stays in the body for an entire year. During that time, you can't have even a single drink.

The chemical is illegal in the United States, but it's legal in Poland and other parts of Eastern Europe. So I had it done. They injected it into my butt, and it made my body completely intolerant of alcohol. For the next year, if I had even one drink, I'd throw up. I would start sweating; my face would get red — a horrible experience.

Or so they tell me.

I never actually got the chemical reaction. From that moment on February 14th, I never had another drink. Not because I was scared of the consequences, but because this time, I really was done with it. The injection was just to keep me accountable.

But I also knew I wasn't the only one who needed to be held accountable. Long before I fell into my own bad habits, I'd seen firsthand what alcoholism does and the destruction it can cause.

That's why, when I went to get the injection, I asked my best friend (who is like a brother) to come with me and get it too. We were in the same boat. And now, our accountability would be to each other. Together, we would break the cycle and establish new patterns for ourselves.

No Stages

When I drank, I compared myself to my friend. I told myself that as long as I wasn't at the point where he was, I was still OK. But now I realize something: The articles I read gave me patterns and behaviors that I could recognize in my best friend and in myself. But when it comes to "stages" of alcoholism — there aren't any. You either are an alcoholic, or you're not. And my friend and I both were. Both are. We may be sober, but the healing never stops.

And it didn't matter if I was still at "Stage 1" while my friend had progressed to "Stage 3." That didn't make me any less in need of help. And it didn't give me license to wait until I was at a later stage before seeking that help. If you're on the path to destruction, it doesn't matter how far along you are. You need to get off.

As soon as you recognize those destructive patterns, those signs of addiction in yourself, you need to take steps to move past them. The sooner you can heal, the better off you'll be. But the longer you wait, the more difficult it gets, and the more harm you'll cause along the way, both to yourself and to others.

BEING OBJECTIVE

So, how do you recognize those self-destructive patterns? I was lucky. Having done the research for someone else gave me the capacity to look at things objectively. I already knew firsthand what the signs looked like, so it made it easier to see them in myself. Not that I didn't still try to deny them, but making that connection between what I knew objectively and what I saw myself doing made it harder to ignore.

Objectivity is the key. You can always make excuses for your behavior. "I'm getting drunk to celebrate the fact that my divorce is finalized." "I'm drinking every day because I'm on vacation." It's only when you look at yourself through an objective lens that you can get past those excuses and see yourself for who you really are — problems, addictions, self-destructive behaviors, and all.

Any good athlete knows that an objective look at yourself is the only way to improve your performance. The best ones record themselves during games or competitions and play back the videos the next day — often over and over again — to observe and critique what they did right and what they did wrong.

Of course, there's no game tape for your life. In the real world, you can't just play back a recording of the things you do and analyze them. But you can take stock of what you did today and what you didn't do and ask yourself why. Why did you make the choices you did, and how did those choices affect those around you? What could you have done differently? How will making different choices tomorrow lead to better outcomes?

Social media can be a good tool for this. A lot of platforms show you memories of what you were doing and what you were posting a year ago, two years ago, etc. How does where you were then compare with where you are now? Do you notice any of the same patterns? Did you make any promises that, looking back, you realize you didn't keep?

Perspective changes everything. By observing yourself from an outside standpoint, you can change your entire view of who you are, what you've done, and what you need to do. The things you've done in the past don't need to define your future. You can change them and make new decisions that will take you off the path to destruction that you're on and send you in a new direction.

FINDING THE PAIN

Self-reflection is not an easy process. In fact, it can be downright painful — like an injection that causes your body literally to reject the thing you've grown to depend on. But if you want to grow and evolve, you need to be able to face that pain. As the saying goes, "No pain, no gain."

If comfort is stagnation, then pain is growth. If comfort holds you hostage, pain is the beginning of the path

IF COMFORT IS STAGNATION, THEN PAIN IS GROWTH. IF COMFORT HOLDS YOU HOSTAGE, PAIN IS THE BEGINNING OF THE PATH TO FREEDOM. to freedom. Pain is what allows you to redefine your soul. You need to face that pain until it no longer cripples you. Only then will you be able to break out of your comfort zone and enter the next phase of your evolution.

THE JOURNEY IS THE ZEITGEIST, NOT THE DESTINATION

CASH RICH

When you're rich, you may be worth a lot of money, but it can still be hard to get your hands on that money, especially if you need a large amount quickly. That was my problem in 2008 when, though I owned all sorts of apartment buildings, I didn't have the ready cash to pay the people I owed.

If I hadn't been able to pull myself out of that situation, I could have lost everything. Not only that, but both my family and I could have gotten hurt. I didn't ever want to be in that position again.

So, after that, I changed the way I did business. I focused on making sure I had enough cash in reserve to do whatever I needed to do. I also focused on paying off my mortgages so I wouldn't owe anything to anyone anymore.

That's how it went for the next few years. I focused on high-leverage investments: high risk, high reward. I used other people's money to buy new properties, and I paid them back as quickly as possible with the rents from those properties. And it worked. I was cash rich. I was completely set and could do whatever I wanted.

A Difference of Opinion

Of course, my lawyers, my CPAs, my business-savvy friends, and everyone else who knew about investments told me I was an idiot.

"You can't keep doing this," they would say to me. "Sure, you make a lot of money, but the amount you'll end up paying in taxes is ridiculous."

I didn't care. I had cash, and I had property. Whatever else happened, I could deal with it. If I kept enough in reserve, then paying a little bit more in taxes was doable. But without that extra cash on hand, I could get caught with my pants down again. "I'd rather owe the money to Uncle Sam than to a bunch of guys who will break my windows if something goes wrong," I told them.

But then it came time to actually pay those taxes.

"What's the damage?" I asked my attorney one day in 2017, as we were going over my financials.

"You owe $1.5 million," he told me. It was a little steep, but nothing I couldn't handle.

"For the year?" I asked.

"For the quarter," he replied. My jaw dropped to the floor. $1.5 million for the quarter. That came to $6 million a year. Could I afford it? Technically, yeah. But it was a huge chunk out of my cash reserves and a much bigger number than I'd been prepared to hand over. I was pissed off.

And then the devil started talking again.

"Jarek, you idiot," the voice said. "He tried to tell you. Everybody tried to tell you. But you don't listen. You think you're so high and mighty. You think you know better than everyone else. You don't. And now you've made a rookie mistake."

Restructuring

Those feelings of Not Enoughness started creeping in again. And it was true, I'd screwed up. I knew how to make money, but there were people who knew a lot more than I did about the details of keeping that money, including the ins and outs of tax law. My attorney owned six offices himself and had just sold one. He knew his stuff. There were people who were smarter than me, and I was paying those people to help me make better decisions. But I didn't listen to them because I was too busy listening to myself.

After getting blindsided by my tax bill, I decided to regroup. There had to be a way to have it all: plenty of cash reserves, not owing a bunch of money to a bunch of people, AND taxes that weren't through the roof. And with the advice of my attorney and my CPA, I found a solution.

Instead of having a lot of little mortgages, I would have just one big loan. I'd get the loan through my life insurance, which offered a great 30-year fixed interest rate — a lot lower than the average mortgage rate at the time. Collateral on the loan was a single, 280-unit apartment community.

That loan paid off the mortgage on every single other property. After that, I owned everything free and clear. And if anything ever happened, and I couldn't pay off the loan, the only thing they could take would be those 280 units.

CUSHION OR OPPORTUNITY?

By 2019, without all of those mortgages to pay off, I found myself with an extra $40 million. If I was looking to be cash-rich, this was it. I could leave this money in the bank and never have to worry about anything else (the interest alone was huge). But then, all the cash flow from the paid-off properties was much, much bigger. All of this cash awakened the giant within me... it "poked the bear," as they say.

I was used to working hard, to driving myself. I didn't use money as a cushion. I used it as a tool, as an opportunity. Now, an extra $40 million had dropped into my lap, and it was just going to sit in the bank doing nothing? I could turn it into so much more than that!

On the other hand, why did I want more? Didn't I have enough? More than enough?

I went back and forth for a long time. One side of me said, "Pull the trigger on the new investment. Pull the trigger. Pull the trigger." And the other side said, "I have enough. I have enough. I have enough."

When Is It Enough?

Finally, I did what I often do when I'm having trouble with a decision. I asked Raul. I called him from my car, and we talked as I drove down the highway.

"I don't need this," I told him. "I have everything I need. But I still have this drive to keep going. When is enough ever Enough?"

Raul looked at me through the screen. "Never," he said.

That was all I needed to hear. I pulled the money out of the bank as soon as I could and went back to work. I started building new portfolios, making new investments, buying new real estate. Six months later, I bought over 1,000 units in Jacksonville. By the time COVID hit in 2020, I was cash rich again and could get any property I wanted for just a few cents on the dollar.

But then, as I alluded to earlier, there was the other thing... I had way more money than I could use. It took me a long time to reinvest the money. I gained thousands of new units but the headaches started all over again. It took me out of retirement. It got me searching for more wealth, which wasn't really what I wanted to do.

WHAT ARE YOU CHASING?

There are two different ways to see the concept of It's Never Enough. One is like an addict: chasing the next high, the next fix, the next deal, hoping that's the one that will bring you what you're looking for. Hoping that finally, it will be Enough, and never getting there.

Especially given my own struggles with addiction, some people might see my decision to go back to work that way. They'd tell me to be happy with what I have instead of constantly chasing more. They'd say to me that, of course, $40 million is enough. What more could I possibly want?

But as you grow and heal, you begin to see it differently. $40 million may be enough, but it isn't Enough. If you're chasing money to give you that feeling of Enoughness, then you're going to be disappointed. It was never about the money, and no magic amount is ever going to give you what you need. It's always been about the journey. That's where the magic happens. That's where we learn. That's where we grow.

If I'd just left that $40 million in the bank and spent the rest of my life living off of the interest, I would never have been satisfied because I would have been giving up on myself. I would have been denying that drive to keep going and admitting that, even though I was only in my mid-40s, my life was basically over. I had nothing more to do and nothing more to chase.

Raul helped me understand that we need to keep moving forward, even when we can't see the destination. Sometimes, we just need to take that leap of faith. The past is gone, and the future's not here yet. But the present moment is where everything happens. That's where we need to live.

There's nothing wrong with planning for the future, of course. We all need to do that. But there's a difference between planning for the future and living for the future. Leaving that $40 million in the bank would have been living for the future — keeping it hidden away for something I might need later on. Meanwhile, in the present, that money was a $40 million opportunity, and to let it sit there would have been to ignore that opportunity.

THE DESTINATION IS NEVER ENOUGH. BUT THE JOURNEY IS ENOUGH.

If you spend all your time living for the future, you miss the opportunities in the present — until one day, you look around, and those opportunities are in the past. And once they're gone, they don't come back. That's why it's so important never to stop chasing them.

The destination is never enough. But the journey is Enough.

THE HERO

MY SELF-IMPOSED DELUSION

I gave up swimming for 28 years.

Why? Because I told myself that I lost my childhood to it. I told myself that it contributed to my unhappiness and my Not Enoughness. I could never swim fast enough or well enough or beat the best. My dad reminded me of that, and so did my coaches.

But that was all crazy. The truth is that swimming, for me, is therapy. It is one of my favorite things to do. And when I gave it up for almost three decades, I now realize that it could have really helped me through all of those tough times.

Swimming could have been my therapy all along.

What I told myself about swimming had so much power over me that I wouldn't even get close to a pool when my kids were young. Countless times, they wanted me to take them to the pool, but I would tell them no.

So selfish. Kids love going to the pool. I wish I would have listened.

It seems we all do that with someone or something in our lives. We tell ourselves a story about it that is completely delusional, but we believe it. And what's worse is that the story we are telling ourselves is actually contributing to our trauma. All of this is self-imposed. No one is doing it to us; we are doing that to ourselves.

So, yeah, once again, I was my own worst enemy.

YOU'RE THE HERO ON YOUR JOURNEY

We're each the protagonist of our own life story, right? That story includes all of our challenges, triumphs, and growth.

Recognizing yourself as the hero of your life journey empowers you to take control, make meaningful choices, and live with purpose. Understanding and embracing this perspective can transform your approach to life's experiences, encouraging resilience, self-discovery, and fulfillment.

We all go through life's many stages — the call to adventure, facing trials, receiving guidance, achieving transformation, and returning home with newfound wisdom.

That's what swimming became for me — a return home. And it helped tremendously with my personal growth over the last ten years.

So, how did I bring swimming back into my life? The Ironman competition.

For years and years, people kept telling me to try a triathlon. I enjoyed running and biking.

But there is no triathlon without swimming, and my mental problem with swimming always prevented me from doing one.

However, after much thought and consideration, in 2014, I finally went back to the pool. It must have been my competitive nature. And just an intuition. I can't really explain it. Possibly some divine intervention. But I can tell you that the moment I hit the water, it all came back to me.

In an instant, I realized what swimming really was for me. It was therapy. It brought me peace. It was a gift in my life, not a noose, not a bad thing at all. And I was good at it! In the water, I was truly free and could shut out the outside world any time I wanted to.

So, over the last 10 years, with all the Ironman competitions and all the practicing, I can now say that swimming has helped me get back to who I always was. It has truly been a big part of my therapy.

And I'll have it for the rest of my life.

The Journey Has 100 Milestones Along the Way

Every hero's journey begins with a call to adventure — an opportunity or challenge that asks you to step out of your comfort zone. In your life, this call might manifest as a career change, a personal goal, a new relationship, or the pursuit of a passion.

Embracing this call requires courage and a willingness to embrace uncertainty. By acknowledging and answering your call to adventure, you set the stage for personal growth and discovery, like I did with swimming (and so many other things).

The journey is not complete without obstacles and trials. These challenges are essential for growth as they test us. Whether facing external difficulties such as financial struggles, health issues, or interpersonal conflicts, or internal battles like self-doubt, fear, or what I call Not Enoughness, overcoming these trials is what it's all about. Working through them, we can develop resilience, learn from mistakes, and emerge stronger and more capable.

The hero's journey is ultimately about transformation. I could never fully be transformed in my life unless I rediscovered my life's passions and joys. Swimming was one of those things for me. What is it for you?

The Inner Journey is More Important than the Outer Journey

The journey is hard! But it is worth it.

At the end of the day, you've got to believe in your own potential and worth. Self-belief is the foundation upon which all heroic actions are built. It involves recognizing your strengths, acknowledging your achievements, and having faith in your ability to overcome challenges.

Cultivating self-belief requires positive self-talk, setting achievable goals, and celebrating your progress, no matter how small. By consistently reinforcing your self-worth, you build the confidence to pursue your dreams and navigate your journey with resilience and determination.

Recognizing yourself as the hero of your life journey is a powerful and transformative perspective. It empowers you to embrace challenges, seek growth, and live with purpose and authenticity. By understanding the stages of the hero's journey, cultivating self-belief, making empowered choices, and living authentically, you can navigate your path with resilience and determination.

As the hero of your story, you not only enrich your own life but also inspire and uplift those around you. Embrace your role as the hero and embark on your journey with confidence, courage, and a sense of adventure, knowing that you have the power to shape your destiny and create a life that is uniquely yours.

You got this!

THE GUIDE

SEEKING TOTAL ESCAPE

I hated the taste of Jack Daniels. When I drank, I would always drink beer. But eventually, it reached the point where beer wouldn't do it for me anymore. So, I started keeping a bottle of whiskey next to my bed.

In a previous chapter, I compared the difference between getting drunk on hard liquor in Poland and having a Corona in Chicago to swimming with weights that pull you under vs. swimming in the Great Salt Lake (Baltic Sea), where you can't help but float. But what if you want to be pulled under?

Beer took forever to get me drunk. With it, I was floating on the Great Salt Lake. But I wanted to be pulled under. For that, I needed the weights. I needed a total escape. So I started drinking that god-awful whiskey and chased it with Coke, just so that I could get drunk as quickly as possible.

A Difficult Journey

When I filed for divorce and gave up drinking from September 2019 through July 2020, I knew I needed to do it. Appearances matter, especially in court, and any misstep, any sign of being out of control or irresponsible, and I could have lost access to my kids.

But that was also one of the most difficult times in my life. Filing for divorce was my decision, but that didn't make it any less difficult.

All I wanted to do was sedate myself and be numb to everything that was going on around me. It was so much easier to deal with problems when I was drunk. But instead, I had to face it sober.

It was especially hard when I was hanging out with my friends. A lot of them still drank, and when we were together, that's what they did. I was the only one not drinking. The more I saw the people around me drink, the more I wanted a drink myself, and I knew I couldn't have one. I knew if this went on, I would fall off the wagon and ruin my divorce. I didn't need friends to drink with me. I needed friends who would help me and support me.

Help Comes to the Door

That's when Libor showed up at my door. Libor was my CFO, as well as a good friend. He had quit drinking too, and his journey had been pretty rough. Now, he was on the right path, though, and trying to be there for his family. In fact, he had a newborn daughter at home — just three days old.

That's why it was such a surprise when he told me he was coming to stay with me.

"Just for a few days," he said. "Just to help you out. It seems like you need somebody."

"Doesn't your family need you?" I asked.

"I talked to my wife about it," he told me. "We agreed that this is where I need to be right now. She told me not to come home until I know that you're safe and you're OK. Meanwhile, YOUR family needs you to be sober. So, let's be sober together."

Libor wasn't my only support. My 16-year-old daughter had left the house with me and lived with me full-time. She was my rock and the purpose for me to maintain a household and a certain level of normality. She was my ride or die. A number of my friends also started coming by regularly to hang out, to check in, and to stay for a few days or a few weeks.

There was Bogdan, my long-time confidante, IT guy, and next-door neighbor. He would come over just about every day. He would see how I was doing, and then we would talk for a while. My other friends would give him breaks every now and then, but if no one else was there, Bogdan would be over to help me out and give me the strength I needed.

And then there was my best friend, Batman. He was in Poland when all of this happened, so he couldn't just come over to the house like the others. But he would call me, and we'd talk for hours. Six hours a day, every day, we would talk. He was there for me like nobody else. Even though Poland is six hours ahead of Florida, he always had time for me when I needed him. In February, his son was born — my godson. Batman still called me from the hospital, and we talked.

THE CHALLENGES OF ISOLATION

When COVID happened, that was when I needed my friends the most. With everything shut down, I had fewer distractions and fewer ways of escape — which made the bottle look that much more appealing. I sank into despair. We were all supposed to be isolated, but my friends kept coming over because they knew I needed them.

And Raul was there for me too. On FaceTime with me, hour after hour, day after day, he helped me through and kept me going when I most wanted to quit.

There are friends who are there when you need them, and there are friends who are there when they need you. When you feel like you're Not Enough, you start wondering which friends fall into which category. I've talked already about how difficult it was for me to trust and open up to people.

Raul's boot camp helped me get past that, but even so, when you're at the Bottom of the Bottom, it's easy to start thinking that you don't have any real friends — which then makes it easy to close yourself off again. You can't imagine anyone caring about you enough to help you through the really big stuff. You worry that if you ask, you'll just be a burden. But then they surprise you.

That's the thing about hard times. It can make you doubt yourself, but it can also show you the best of people. I was completely blown away by the love and support I got from my friends. People showed up I never would have expected to hear from. People went out of their way for me in ways I couldn't have imagined. I can honestly say I wouldn't be here today if it weren't for them.

Then, in May of that year, I met Jessica, and she became my rock. My friends went home, and Jessica became the one I was able to lean on, who helped get me through — and she's been doing it ever since.

A Little Help from My Friends

Toxic masculinity is thinking you have to do everything alone. It's the belief that if you have to ask for help, you're weak. I thought that for a long time. That's why it was such a shock to me that so many of my friends went to such lengths to help me when I needed it.

"But Jarek, you would have done the same for them!" others would tell me.

That's just it: At that time, I probably wouldn't have.

For most of my life, I was the "pull yourself up by your bootstraps" guy. If a friend told me about a problem they were having, I wouldn't say, "How can I help?" I'd say, "Quit whining!" I had no empathy at all. If I'd seen someone else going through the things that I ended up going through myself, I wouldn't have given them the time of day.

You're an alcoholic? Quit drinking. You're depressed? Just get out of bed. How hard can it be?

But when I was there myself, I needed help. And I count myself very lucky that my friends weren't like me. I have the kind of friends who would actually be there for me, through thick and thin, and see me through those dark times.

The Brotherhood

It's true that you're the hero of your own story. And every hero needs a guide. Raul has been my guide for years. He set me on the right path and got me through some of the darkest times in my life.

Yeah, he's my life coach, and that's what I pay him for. But the way he's been there for me goes far beyond a simple coach-client relationship. You don't sit on FaceTime with someone for hours, day after day, talking them down from the ledge because they're paying you. You do it because you care about them.

And Raul's not the only one. Libor was my guide, helping me navigate sobriety as a sober person himself. My neighbor, Bogdan, was my guide when he came over to check on me. My good friend, Batman, was my guide, as he talked to me six hours a day, every day, to make sure I had what I needed. And my friend from the brotherhood, Daniel B, stayed with me many times and walked me through the stages of a divorce. He went through a divorce two years earlier and introduced me to my first ayahuasca ceremony, which completely changed my life.

These people aren't just my guides. They're *my brothers.* They're my support system. They're the ones I can count on when I'm in crisis and the ones who help me on my journey.

But my brothers taught me that support is a two-way street. Through their caring for me, I realized that if any of them needed help or guidance from me, it was my job to be there for them too. Because I owe them for the help they gave me? No. Because I care about them and want to make sure they're taken care of, just like they care about me. Because I know what it's like to be lost in the darkness, and if I can be a guide to others, if my experiences, my assistance, or just my presence can help lead others out of that darkness, then I'll do everything I can. That's the reason I'm writing this book. I want to help people I haven't even met — including you.

LEANING ON EACH OTHER

So, ask yourself: Who are the guides in your life? Who are the people you can lean on for support? Are you strong enough to ask them for the help you need?

Then ask: Who needs YOU as a guide? Who can you be there for? And do they have the strength to ask you for what they need? If not, what are some ways you can be there for them anyway and support them on their journey?

We all need each other in this world. Everyone needs someone, and the more you isolate yourself, the harder it is. We're designed to lean on each other, even if we're conditioned to think that doing that is weak. We think that we have to do it all on our own, but the more we shut out the people around us, the more we feel like we're Not Enough.

That's why you need to surround yourself with people you care about and people you can count on. They're the ones who can show you that you ARE Enough — and that you're worthy of love. Don't be afraid to talk to them about what you need, about what you're going through, about your experiences — and about their experiences and what they're going through, too. Because the only way we're getting through this life is together.

SURROUND YOURSELF WITH THE RIGHT PEOPLE

FROM THE GROUND UP

I built my real estate empire in Colorado from the ground up. I started with four units and gradually kept adding more over time until, eventually, I had over a thousand. And while I've talked about just purchasing the units and letting the rent come in, there's actually a lot more to it than that. It's a business, like any other.

Before you can collect rent, you need to make sure there are people to collect rent from. And to do that, you need to make sure you have a place where they'll want to live. You need to make sure things are running properly. And you need to make sure you hire the right people to manage the day-to-day operations of each of your properties.

That's what I did in Colorado. From the very beginning, I was there, turning those units into well-oiled machines and making sure everything was done right. And it paid off. The reason I made so much money is because the apartments were always full. There was a waiting list to get in. People knew me, and they knew my properties. They knew they were places worth renting, and so they wanted to rent them.

Even when I retired from the business, the infrastructure I had put into place was still there. It was still being run the same, and the apartments were still very much in demand. I took it for granted that at any given time, every unit would be filled and generating income.

BACK IN BUSINESS

Then, in 2019, I found myself with that extra $40 million, and I went back to work. I started purchasing units again. Only I wasn't in Colorado anymore. I was living in Florida. And I wasn't just starting out anymore, buying a few units at a time as I could afford them. So, I purchased 1,000 units in Jacksonville.

At first, things were fine. Money was coming in, and it seemed like business as usual. But when I looked at the reports for my new properties, I saw that there were over three hundred vacancies.

Everyone told me it was nothing to worry about. When you have 1,000 units, a few vacancies are to be expected. And I still had seven hundred units bringing in money, after all. But I couldn't accept that. In Colorado, if I had two vacancies at once, it was an indication that there was an issue. To have three hundred? It was a serious problem.

Bought, Not Built

The problem was that along with the 1,000 units, I had bought a lot of problems.

This was a different scenario from Colorado. Remember, there, I had bought a few units at a time. While I was adding more properties, I was also building an infrastructure to support the business. But in Florida, I hadn't built that infrastructure; I had bought it. Unlike my situation in Colorado, where two vacancies were an issue, this Florida infrastructure was one in which three hundred vacancies were considered normal.

Another problem was that I was a newcomer to the Jacksonville real estate scene. In Colorado, I was always very hands-on. I didn't just create the infrastructure. I created the culture. I myself found tenants to put into the units. As a result, I had a reputation. Everyone knew me, and they knew my units were the best.

But when I came on the scene in Jacksonville and bought 1,000 units out of the gate, suddenly, I was just some rich guy from Miami. Since I was buying so many at a time, they assumed I was just trying to make a quick buck — that I didn't actually care about the apartments or the tenants in them. And if I didn't care, why should anyone else?

They were wrong, of course. I did care. But it's also true that when you buy 1,000 units at once, it's a lot harder to be hands-on. I would come around once a month to take a look at what was going on, but when I was juggling so many at once, I didn't really have the time to be there more than that.

I also had problems with the people working for me. In Colorado, I built my team over time. I found people I trusted to do the work and keep things running. But in Jacksonville, most of the employees were already there, and I didn't know much about them. I assumed they'd been vetted for their jobs and possessed the skills to keep things running smoothly.

It turned out that many of them had their jobs not because they were qualified and experienced but because they knew someone else in the company. Some were incompetent, while others outright stole from me.

Of course, whenever anything like this happened, I would fire them. But then their friends in the office would hire them right back without my knowledge, and the cycle would continue. And as long as it did, nothing was ever going to get better.

MAKING CHANGES

It was clear things had to change. I started by bringing some of the people I trusted from Colorado to Jacksonville to help run things. The stealing and the cronyism stopped, but we still had 300 vacancies.

I didn't know what to do. I was so used to things in Colorado running smoothly, but now, in Jacksonville, I felt like nothing was making a difference.

Wow, I thought to myself. *I never realized how lucky I was in Colorado.*

And then I stopped in my tracks. As I've said before, I hate it when people look at my success and call me lucky. It's never been about luck. In fact, I've had to fight through some pretty unlucky circumstances to get where I am. I didn't get lucky. I worked my tail off.

Now, here I was, buying 1,000 units and expecting everything to be the same. But I hadn't put in the work. I hadn't built this from the ground up and the inside out. If I was going to succeed here, I was going to need a complete overhaul.

With that in mind, we started making more changes. Vanessa, my amazing Chief Operations Officer, led the charge. She looked at the problems we had in Jacksonville and implemented new standards and new policies to fix those problems. She decided that to step up, we needed to be on the cutting edge. So, we outfitted the entire business with new technology. We put in a new software system to handle the data. We switched to a new email system to ensure better communication between staff members. We gave them company iPads so they'd always have whatever they needed at their fingertips.

We trained our new staff to use the new technology and navigate the new infrastructure. Once it started working, we had plans to send them to Colorado to implement the new changes there, too. The problems in Colorado were a little different. The business was actually getting too big there. An overhaul was due, and I thought maybe the new technology could help. So, I figured I'd send my Jacksonville guys over with software and iPads to train the staff and get things where they needed to be.

Finding What Works

In the end, I did send my Jacksonville guys to Colorado, but it wasn't to teach. It was to learn.

The new infrastructure didn't work. The new technology didn't work. I finally realized I didn't need some fancy new business model or cutting-edge new technology. I needed what I'd always had: capable people I knew and trusted to do what worked. In the end, what we were missing was *the culture*. Once I found a way to implement the culture of Colorado into my Jacksonville apartments, things started to get better.

I started looking around for consultants — people who understood company culture and could help me change it. I looked at a lot of different companies until, finally, I found some people who shared my values regarding business and staff. I hired them, and I worked with them, and over the course of a year or two, we managed to turn things around.

BUILDING RELATIONSHIPS

Hard work is important. I never would have gotten anywhere in Jacksonville, in Colorado, or anywhere else, without working for it. But no matter how hard you work, you can't do it alone. That's why it's just as important to surround yourself with the right people. You need to find people who share your vision and who want to build with you — partners in every sense of the word.

That's what I had in Colorado. I had people I trusted, people I'd worked with for years who had helped me build

HARD WORK IS IMPORTANT. BUT NO MATTER HOW HARD YOU WORK, YOU CAN'T DO IT ALONE.

my business from the ground up. That's why things worked: because they knew the ropes as well as I did. It was more than just a staff. It was a community.

And that's exactly why things didn't work at first in Jacksonville. I didn't have that community. Everyone was just looking out for themselves. Some might have been looking out for their friends, but at the expense of the business rather than to its benefit.

WHAT DO YOU CARE ABOUT?

We take care of the people and things that we care about. That quality is what made Colorado such a success and also what made Jacksonville such a toxic environment. In Colorado, we cared about the team, we cared about the business, and we cared about the tenants. In Jacksonville, they cared about getting money, doing favors, and staying secure in their own jobs.

In a situation like that, the only way to fix things is to cut out those toxic elements and build a real community of trust and respect in its place. You need to create boundaries. If that doesn't work, you may need to create moats. Whatever it takes to stop that toxicity from getting in and ruining what you have or what you're trying to do.

But if you can do that — if you can eliminate the toxic people and instead surround yourself with people you can trust, people who can help, people you can build with — then there's no limit to what you can do or the kind of success you can have.

WHO'S BUILDING YOU UP?

DENYING GOD

On a bright Sunday morning, maybe eight years ago, I was picking up my (second) wife and kids from church to take them to Broncos Stadium for a game. As we drove along I-25, the kids were talking about what they'd learned in church that day. Then, the conversation turned into an argument about something. I don't remember what, but it got on my nerves. Finally, I just lashed out.

"How do you believe all of this stuff? It's all garbage!"

My wife looked at me in horror. "What's garbage?" she asked.

"God, the priests, all of it," I replied. "None of it's real!"

"How can you say something like that?" my wife asked. "Especially with the kids in the car! How can you say God isn't real?"

"There's no God!" I said. "The priests are fakes! It's all just a big con!"

I couldn't believe this was coming out of my mouth. But I just kept going, laying into God and religion and everything else.

Struggling with Catholicism

Growing up in Poland, I was raised Catholic. Religion was a part of my life for as long as I could remember.

But something had happened to me over the years. I looked around, and I didn't see God anymore. I didn't see what God had done in my life. I saw what I had done. And I saw a lot of terrible things being done in the world in the name of God and the name of religion. People use it not as a tool to do good in the world but as a shield to hide and justify whatever they want to do.

I also struggled with Catholicism as a husband and father. How can a priest tell me how to be a good father when he doesn't have any children of his own? How can a priest tell me how to be a good husband when he's never been married? I wouldn't go to a personal trainer who never gets off the couch. I wouldn't ask for business advice from someone who's never run a business.

And if priests represent God, then I couldn't see how God could be relevant to my life. So, I decided it had to be all a lie.

THE PEAK AND THE FALL

At this point in my life, I was at my peak. I had money, I had success, I had a family, I had everything I had ever wanted. I was on top of the world. And looking back, I realize it was also the moment when things began to crumble.

A few years later, I had lost — not everything, but more than I ever dreamed I would. I'd just filed for divorce from my second wife, my kids didn't want to see me, and I was still trying to recover from the skiing accident that had almost taken my leg and could have left me unable to walk.

And during this time, I found myself lying on the grass one night, looking up at the sky, and all I could think was, *Why me, God? Why me?*

How could God let this happen to me? How could He take so much from me? How could He make me suffer like this? What did I do to deserve all of this pain?

That's when I realized: When I had everything, I was making fun of religion and telling my kids, "There is no God!" But now, at the bottom of the bottom, suddenly, it was, "Why me, God?"

A Wakeup Call

That moment was the beginning of my coming back to my faith.

It took time. I had to get my ego in check. It was the part of me that thought that my being on top was just because I was so great and so deserving. That part believed I was untouchable and could do no wrong.

Was my fall from grace a punishment for that ego? I think it was more of a wake-up call from God. It was a reminder that I was not the one in charge. My skiing accident, my divorces, and almost losing all the money my friends had invested through me — these things were humbling experiences. And they taught me that when things start to go wrong, I need to trust in God rather than myself.

But I couldn't learn those things while I was doing well. I had to go through the hard stuff first. It's just like physical training. A workout regime is designed literally to tear your body down, piece by piece, so it can rebuild itself stronger, faster, and with more stamina.

It's the same with your spiritual journey. Just as you learn from failure, not success, you grow by going through hardship, not by being comfortable. And my hardships have served me well.

Connecting with God

Now, I pray every morning, asking God to forgive my belief that I've got my act together and nothing can hurt me. And for my thinking that I was the one running my own life. It's a reminder I need daily. As soon as I start thinking I'm the one in charge of my life and my circumstances, that's when I start drowning. And God is the only one with a life raft.

As soon as I started praying and meditating — staying in contact with God and attuned to what He wants for me, not what I want for myself — things started to change. Not my outer circumstances but my inner being. Praying to God isn't like rubbing a magic lamp and making a wish granted by a genie. For me, it was an awakening of myself.

Once I had that awakening, it was like **switching to a whole new frequency**. My energy completely shifted. It allowed me to open up and be more vulnerable — to acknowledge that I can't do everything. It gave me the strength to face the things that were plaguing me in my life, with God's help and with the help of the people around me.

I also was able to start connecting with a lot better quality people: the kind of people who would help me out when I'm in need and be there for me when times are dark.

CALLED TO SERVE

That time spent with God has also helped me to understand better who I am ,what I'm here for, and why I have the success that I do in the first place.

God didn't put me on this Earth just to be a rich jerk. I'm not here to make myself better. I'm not here to prove to others how great I am or how much I can do. I'm here so God can use me to serve others.

I've always tried to be a giver. I use what I have to help others and provide them with what they need. But once I reconnected with God, I realized that I wasn't giving to my full potential. There was so much more I could do. When I have plenty and others have so little, I need to do what I can to help them out and lift them up. And what I can do is often a lot more than what I actually do. But over the years, I've started to realize how much potential I really have for serving others, for helping the people around me.

That potential is *unlimited*.

When I was working for myself, setting goals for my own personal gain, there were always limits. Make a million dollars, a hundred million, a billion. Qualify for the Olympics. Do the Ironman. Win the Ironman. It's all bound by human limits.

But with God's help, there's no limit to the number of people I can help or the amount of good that I can do. It's infinite. With God, whatever is needed, I can do.

FINDING YOUR PATH

Now, this isn't me telling you that you need to become a Christian or that following my beliefs is the only way to get the healing you need. There are all different religions. People believe in all different ideas of God. It's not for me to say which way is best. A lot of it just has to do with where you were born. I was born in Poland, so I was raised Catholic. If I'd been born in India, I might have been raised Hindu. Somewhere else, I might have been a Buddhist or a Muslim. Though I was born in one place and you were born in another, that doesn't mean I'm right and you're wrong.

Even Christians have different beliefs, different types of faith, and different ways of practicing it. Mine are what work for me. They might not work for you, and that's fine. But the important thing is to get in touch with a higher power: something that you can have faith in, something that you can let guide you.

The important thing is to recognize that you can't do it all yourself. Whatever you're doing, you AREN'T doing it all yourself. When you become successful, especially when you're young, it's so easy to get an ego. You think, "I must be better than everyone else. I must deserve this. Why else would I have all of this?"

But I've said it before, and I'll say it again: As soon as you start thinking that way, you're setting yourself up for a fall. If you try to do it alone or claim you've done it all alone, you'll just end up crashing.

But when you open yourself up to a higher power to guide you, to work through you, there's no limit to what you can do. Not only that, it will change your whole idea of what success even is. Suddenly, things are happening that you never thought were possible. Not just more than you thought possible but a completely different view of the life you're living and what you can do with it. Divine power is infinite. And with it, you can do more than just anything. With God's help, you can do *everything.*

WHO ARE YOU BUILDING UP?

THE PROVIDER

While I was growing up, my father's job wasn't to spend time with me or to give me help and advice. His job was to work and bring home the paycheck that would provide for the family. Taking care of the kids was my mother's job.

My father was at work all day. When he came home, he'd read the newspaper and take a nap. After that, he'd watch TV — which meant the rest of us had to be quiet so he could pay attention to whatever he was watching.

He never did dishes or cleaned the house. He had his job, and he did it. When he wasn't doing that job, he was entitled to rest and relax. Asking him to spend time with us or help us with something would be infringing on that hard-earned rest and relaxation time.

THE FATHER-DAUGHTER DANCE

Because that father image was what I knew, that's how I was with my kids. I didn't give them my time. I gave them my money. And I felt that was all they should need from me. To ask for anything more would just be entitled.

"Daddy, come with me to the Father-Daughter Dance!" My daughter would ask me this every year.

"Why would I do that?" I asked her.

"It's just a fun thing to do!" she told me.

"I don't have time for dances," I said. "I'm working."

"But all the other dads do it!" she replied.

"Do the other dads make the kind of money that I do?" I asked. "Do their kids live the kind of lives that you do? The reason they have time to take their daughters to Father-Daughter Dances is because they're just sitting around with nothing else to do! But in order to give you the things that I do, I need to work!"

I didn't go to the Father-Daughter Dance that year. Or the next. I wasn't that type of dad, and as far as I was concerned, I shouldn't have to be.

My kids disagreed. They always told me that all they wanted was me. They wanted my time.

"You've got all of this stuff, and you want my time, too?"

They told me they didn't care about the stuff.

"Whatever. Look at this house we live in! Look at the beautiful bikes you ride! Look at your brand-new iPhones! I give you everything. And you want my time, too? You're entitled little brats!"

Entitlement

I called my kids entitled for wanting to spend time with me. The irony was, I was the most entitled person you've ever met. All my success, all the things I had, I took for granted that I deserved them. That they meant I was better than everyone else.

How dare you ask me for my time? My time is more valuable than yours! You can't just have things! You need to earn them!

Did I earn it, though? I worked hard for the money I had, sure. But does that mean I'd earned the right to treat people like crap? To spend all my time on myself instead of with my kids?

I had to learn that when it comes to relationships, what people remember isn't what you do for them. It's how you make them feel. I gave my daughters everything, but I still made them feel like I didn't really care about them. If I hadn't bought them bikes and iPhones, if we lived in a studio apartment instead of a mansion, but I had spent time with them, done things with them, been there for them... I doubt they would have remembered doing without those luxuries, but

> I HAD TO LEARN THAT WHEN IT COMES TO RELATIONSHIPS, WHAT PEOPLE REMEMBER ISN'T WHAT YOU DO FOR THEM. IT'S HOW YOU MAKE THEM FEEL.

I'm certain they would have fond memories of their dad loving them and caring for them.

But the people you love need to see your face. Whether in their good times or dark times — and especially during their dark times — they need to know that you're there for them, no matter what. You need to be a presence in their lives. In order to be a presence, you need to be present.

LEARNING TO BE A HUMAN

Like every other lesson, I had to learn this one the hard way. After I filed for divorce, my eldest daughter ran away and then disowned me. My younger daughter cut me off a few months after that. I blamed my ex-wife for turning them against me, but the truth was, they wanted nothing to do with me because I had shown them, over and over, that I wanted nothing to do with them.

It took Jessica to help me realize how entitled I really was. Just through little things she did. When we'd take a flight somewhere, I'd line up in the special line with the first-class passengers. But she'd just stand in the regular line with the economy passengers.

"Come on," I told her. "Come get in line with First Class!"

"What difference does it make?" she asked. "We're all getting on the same plane, and we're all going to the same place."

On a practical level, I paid the extra money for first class, and it came with certain perks. The problem was that I had fallen into the trap of thinking that because I had that extra money, it made me better than those who didn't, and those extra perks were one of the defining characteristics that separated me from them. But Jessica showed me that none of that mattered. We're all just people.

Learning to Connect

Jessica has also helped me these last few years as I've tried to reconnect with my daughters and rebuild our relationship. I say "rebuild," but in truth, we never had a relationship before. Not really. But I'm trying to build one now — to heal the old wounds, make up for past mistakes, and have a genuine relationship with my daughters based on love and trust — and time.

It's not always an easy task. For one thing, I've realized that I don't know how to talk to my daughters. I was absent from their lives for so long, and I didn't take an interest in the things that they cared about... so I don't know what to talk about.

When I told Jessica this, her advice was simple. "Just ask them questions."

"OK," I said. "Questions about what?"

"About their lives. About what they've got going on. What they're doing, what they're hoping for, what they care about."

"OK," I said. "Like what?"

Jessica sighed. "I'll make you a list."

And she did. She made me a list of questions I can ask my kids when we talk. She also made me a list of general talking points. Things they'd be interested in, things we might have in common, etc. It may seem kind of silly, but it's been a real help! Those questions and talking points have allowed me to connect with my kids in ways I never could before. They've helped me to be present in my kids' lives — which is all they really wanted from me to begin with.

Emotional Intelligence

I've also read books on parenting and connecting with your children. I've talked to therapists too, to try to get past the blocks I spent so many years building up. It's been a real eye-opener, discovering all the work I still have to do.

I'm a smart guy. A big part of my success has come from making smart decisions. But when it comes to emotional intelligence, I'm an idiot. I was raised to think that showing emotions made you weak. You suppress them, you ignore them, you deny them. I was so disciplined in my life, so driven, that I just forced any emotions out.

That meant that for most of my life, there were only two emotions: happy or angry. Sad? Afraid? Disappointed? Depressed? No need for any of those. Not even a capacity for them. They make you weak.

Part of my healing has been exploring my emotions and really understanding them. And the reason I've taken the time to do that is for my kids. For years, I had no idea how much my lack of emotional intelligence was hurting them. Now, I can experience, display, and share my emotions. And I can talk to them about theirs. I can ask them how they're feeling and connect with them over the answers.

JOINING THE DANCE

When my youngest daughter was 11 years old, I finally went with her to the Father-Daughter Dance.

We went, we danced, we had a good time. And after it was over, I cried like a baby. It was such a simple thing, but it was a moment of genuine, emotional connection between us. And I could have had it so much sooner, if only I'd gotten out of my own way for one night and said yes like all the other dads did.

During my kids' whole lives, I had refused to be part of the dance — not just the Father-Daughter dance, but *the dance of life*. The one that connects us all. For years, my daughters begged me to be part of theirs in a hundred different ways. But now, I'm finally ready to join the dance.

My relationship with my daughters is now the best it's ever been — but we still have a long way to go. I'm doing the work, and hopefully, eventually, we'll get there. Like any other kind of healing, though, it's an ongoing process.

And I've told them I'm in it for the long haul. What we're building now, together, is to prepare us for the next ten, twenty, fifty years — so that it only keeps getting stronger, and what happened before will never happen again.

LEAVE A LEGACY OR INHERITANCE

A LIFE SPENT CHASING

I've said before that while I have plenty of mental intelligence, my emotional intelligence is pretty much zero. With a lot of help from those around me, I've learned to be better about it these last few years. Recognizing my emotions and becoming more in touch with them is part of my healing. But it doesn't come naturally, and every step is an uphill battle.

Part of the reason is that my life has always been about chasing goals. I'd have something that I wanted to accomplish, and that's all I would focus on. Nothing else was more important. Whether the goal was making money, training for the Ironman, or recovering from my accident, I didn't have time for anything else.

I'd get so focused on what I was trying to do, what I was working toward, that I'd have no awareness of what was going on around me in the moment. *I don't have time for any of that!* I would think. *I've got more important things to worry about!*

THE IMPORTANT THINGS

The irony, of course, is that a lot of those things that I would shrug off because I was doing something "more important" turned out to be a lot more important than what I was actually doing. Especially since the things I shrugged off included my friends, my family, and especially my kids when they tried to ask me for something or came to me for help.

I was totally focused on my goals, and I was able to get and have everything I needed. So why should I help anyone else? They should just buckle down and do it, like me, instead of bugging other people for help — especially when those people are busy!

Because I thought this way, I was totally unsympathetic to other people's needs and totally out of touch with what anyone else might be feeling. I didn't even understand what emotions they might be having. As I've said, happy or angry. That was all I understood. If someone came to me and told me they were sad? What did I care? I had no time for that. Buck up and quit whining.

THE OPPOSITE OF GREAT

The problem with lacking emotional intelligence is that you also lack the self-awareness to understand why lacking it is a problem or what you need to do to fix it.

And, if you don't understand your own emotions, having empathy becomes impossible. A lack of empathy makes it difficult to help anyone else. When you see things in such simplistic terms as "happy or angry," how can you even recognize what you're missing, much less get help finding it?

The first time I talked with Raul, he asked me what was wrong in my life.

"Nothing," I told him. "I have money. I have a family. I have my health. Every aspect of my life is good."

And then he told me something that blew my mind.

"Good is the opposite of great."

I didn't understand what he meant at first. Isn't bad the opposite of good? Aren't good and great basically the same? Great is better, of course, but good is... well, good! Isn't it?

But if that was true, then being "good" wouldn't have made me so miserable. "Good" is what you are on the surface when you don't know what you are or want to be. "Great" is what you strive for. "Good" is what you settle for.

If you're doing badly, then at least you recognize what the problem is, which puts you in a position to fix it, to do better, to heal. But understanding that requires emotional intelligence that I just didn't have. All I could do was look around at what I had. And by that standard, I was good.

THE PAIN OF ENDURANCE

At that point in my life, I was totally out of touch with my own emotions. Whatever I was feeling, I would push it down, bottle it up. It was just a distraction from working toward my goals.

This was especially true when I was doing the Ironman. When you're training for endurance sports, you're pushing yourself to the limit, to the point where you're in physical pain. All you're thinking about is the physical: how to endure the pain, how to reduce the pain. You don't have the capacity for emotional awareness.

And that's how it went through most of my kids' childhood years. I was so focused on my goals that the negativity around me just got tuned out. None of it mattered. I was a training machine and nothing else — until it all caught up with me.

You can't hide from your emotions forever. And that's what the chase is, at its core. Hiding. It's a distraction. You don't think it's a distraction in the moment. In fact, you might see it as just the opposite. You're pursuing your goal! That's not a distraction; that's laser focus! Nothing could be more important than that! But it acts as a distraction when it gives you that excuse to keep from dealing with any of the other problems in life.

Whatever's going on around you, there's always something more important that you need to deal with. You need a bigger house! You need a better body! You need a faster time! Let someone else handle all the rest. You're totally focused on the chase.

MY SON'S EQ

Now that I'm finally on the right path, the last thing I want is to see the people I love go down the same wrong paths that I did or choose the chase over real emotional connection. So last year, when my son was 13, I brought him to one of Raul's events in the hope that he could learn some of the things that I had.

Toward the end of the event, Raul asked if anyone wanted to come up and talk and share their experiences. My son raised his hand. He took the stage and started talking about emotions, about vulnerability. He started sharing things I never would have been comfortable sharing at his age. And I realized **my son is more emotionally mature than I am.**

When it comes to emotional intelligence, my son is all the things I'm not. He's always aware of his own emotions, which also makes him more aware of the things that are going on around him and the emotions that they cause, both in himself and others.

Like most teenagers, hormones make his emotions go all over the place at times. But he manages to stay in touch with them. Even something as simple as, "I don't like this feeling," or "Yeah! This feeling is the best!" Or "This is causing me anxiety." I didn't know what anxiety was until I was 46 years old — much less be able to talk about it. If you had told me back then, "I think you're suffering from anxiety," I would have just laughed at you.

"Why are we talking about emotions? Are you gay? Are you a woman? Real men don't talk about their feelings!" That was how I was raised, and that was my mindset for a long time. It's taken years to get to the point where I'll let myself feel what I'm feeling. Where I'll let myself cry and really be present in those tears. And I still have a long way to go.

The Right Kind of Legacy

It's clear that my son didn't learn any of this from me. Honestly, I'm not sure where he learned it. He could easily have followed the behaviors he saw in me for most of his life and ended up continuing the same cycles that I got from my parents. I wish I had had the emotional capacity from the beginning to teach him these lessons myself and set the right example.

But the beautiful thing is, he's still at the beginning of his journey. He's advanced, sure, but he still has a long way to go, too. That's just part of growing up and gaining experience. And my hope is that now that I'm learning these things for myself, I can also be there to help guide him.

What kind of legacy do I want to leave for him and my daughters? That's one of the things I thought about *while staring at the gravestone* during Raul's boot camp. I'll leave them plenty of money, sure. But do I want my legacy to be only money? Is that all I am?

What is a legacy, exactly? It's the impact for the future that someone has on the world and other people. It can last a long time. The legacy you create today can span generations. This means you need to be mindful of what that legacy is, where it comes from, and what impact it will have.

We don't always create the legacies we pass on. Sometimes, what our parents give to us, we, in turn, give to our children. That includes everything from generational wealth to family heirlooms to behaviors and mindsets. The things we have, the things we learn, and the things we do can all become cycles that, if left unchecked, will continue long after we're gone.

OUR CYCLES

I broke many of the cycles of my family when I came to the U.S. from Poland. It was a land of new opportunities that allowed me to give my children a better life than either I or my parents had had. Even if I had just had an ordinary, middle-class job, the life I gave my children here would have been far better than what they would have had in Poland.

But this country gave me the opportunity for success beyond anything I could have imagined in Poland and wealth that I can pass on to them and their children and their children's children.

I also carried some of the old cycles with me, though. I repeated my parents' examples of marriage, fatherhood, and motherhood because that was all I knew. And, in doing so, I was continuing the legacy of emotional neglect, of not being present, which I learned from them.

I can leave my children a legacy of wealth — an inheritance, but what about my emotional legacy? What are the cycles I'm creating or continuing with regard to how I treat those around me? Those legacies don't just come from family, either. When my friends stayed with me during my divorce and made sure I was OK, when Raul stayed on calls with me for hours, day after day, and refused to let me give up, they showed me a legacy of caring that I'd never known before — but which I now try to pass on to those around me, by being there for them when they need me.

FINDING WHAT REALLY MATTERS

You can have all the money in the world, but in the end, that's not what matters. That's the distraction. It keeps you from asking the real questions. Did I love the people around me? Was I loved by them? Did I make a difference in this world? Did I use what I have, both physical and spiritual, to give back to others? Did my life mean something?

If your whole life was devoted to making money, then no, it didn't mean anything. If you didn't share that money with those around you or use it to help those in need — if you didn't share yourself: your time and your talents — then no, you didn't make a difference. If you're only focused on the chase, then it's difficult to love those around you or even to love yourself. And if you don't show love to the people around you, then it's difficult for them to love you.

FACING THE PAST, PRESENT, AND FUTURE

Leaving a legacy is about focusing on the future. But to do that, you first have to deal with the past. It's not easy. And at the beginning of your healing, you're tempted just to say, "Leave the past in the past."

You can't leave it in the past. ***But that doesn't mean you should let your past define you.*** Your job is to learn from it. Find meaning in your hardships. Understand why you went through those hard times and use that understanding to change yourself going forward. Your past can make you a better person. Knowing that you did the wrong thing yesterday can help you do the right thing today.

Take the lessons from the past with you but leave the pain of the past behind. If you hang on to the pain, the pain can end up being your legacy. If you don't heal, you can end up passing your toxic mindsets on to your children, which can lead them to the same toxic behaviors, resulting in the same pain.

My marriages looked like my parents' marriage. I learned about being a father from my father. Repeating those same cycles led to the failure of both of my marriages, and for a while, it cost me my relationship with my kids as well. The only way I've been able to rebuild those relationships is by recognizing the pain and mistakes of my past and working to mend them and to do better in the present.

WHAT YOU DO RIGHT NOW IS ALL THAT MATTERS.

Healing is possible. Rebuilding is possible. The past doesn't define you. And your goals for the future shouldn't define you either. **What you do right now is all that matters.**

AN UNEXPECTED COMPANION

Healing is possible. It's not easy. In fact, it may be the most difficult thing you've ever done. Healing will lead you down paths you never thought you could or even should go down. It will feel strange and unfamiliar, and you'll want to resist it. But the more you resist, the harder it is to get through and the harder it will be to heal.

I've talked about how, when I went to Raul's boot camp, I had no idea what I was in for. When I arrived, I had a friend waiting for me, just in case things got too weird and I decided to bail. And believe me, there were times when I thought about bailing.

One of the first things we did as a group was check into our hotel and get our room assignments. We got our keys, walked to our rooms... And as I stopped in front of my door, another guy stopped there with me. As I'm fumbling for my keycard, he's fumbling for his too.

I didn't say anything. I just looked at him. Did he have the wrong room? Did I have the wrong room? I checked my keycard. I had it right. He must be wrong. Should I say something? No, he'd figure it out when his keycard didn't open the...

The door opened. He started hauling his bags inside.

"Hi!" he said to me. "Looks like we're roommates!"

Roommates? What the heck?! I texted Raul immediately.

"How much do I have to pay to get a room to myself?"

"No upgrades," he texted back. "And no switching rooms. This is your room, and this is your roommate for the duration of the boot camp."

"But I don't want a roommate!" I texted him. "I just want to be alone!"

"Trust the process," was the reply.

TRUST THE PROCESS

Raul's boot camp is more than just a camp or a retreat. Healing is not "one size fits all." So, he tailors the experience to the people who sign up. What do they need most in order to help them?

At this point in my life, I was used to being alone. I didn't talk to the people around me. I didn't have time for my friends and family because I was always busy. And I didn't trust most people because I assumed they all just wanted something from me — probably money. I cut myself off and kept myself isolated. So, the thought of being in such close quarters with someone for the duration of the camp made me really uncomfortable.

Raul knew that. He also knew it was just what I needed: to share space with someone I didn't know in order to open up to the world around me. And he knew that I wouldn't listen if he told me that. So, instead, he told me to trust the process.

That's how healing works. A lot of the time, it's uncomfortable, and a lot of the time, you won't understand why. But the only way to grow is if you trust the process. God has a plan for you. He knows where you need to end up and what path you need to take to get there — even when you don't. The path may seem strange and unfamiliar. It's going to be difficult and uncomfortable sometimes. But the more you resist, the harder it is to heal and the more difficult and uncomfortable it becomes. If you just trust the process, you'll end up with more than you ever could have imagined.

WHAT YOU'VE IMAGINED

If you're like me, then you've imagined success: financial, physical, tangible, measurable. You've got your goals, and every ounce of your being is dedicated to achieving them.

You're here for a purpose beyond those goals, though. You're here for more than just yourself and your success. By obsessing over what you want to accomplish in the future, you end up ignoring the person you are right now.

That's why healing and emotional growth are "more than you ever could have imagined." Because the goals you strive for, no matter how lofty they are, are limiting. And when you limit yourself like that, growth becomes impossible. **Instead of obsessing over your goals, become obsessed with being your best self.** Strive for healing. Strive for growth. Make that your mission in life.

And then strive to help others as well. Strive to help them grow and become their best selves. Be there for the people who need you. If you're going to spend your life chasing something, that's what you need to be chasing: the good you can do for the people around you. When that becomes your goal, the possibilities become infinite. There's no limit to the amount of good you can do in this world.

YOUR EMOTIONAL LEGACY

The good we strive for is something we can pass on, too. Seeing the examples set for me by Jessica, Batman, Bodgan, Raul, and my brothers who helped me deal with my divorce and my drinking, showed me how important it is to care for other people.

Now, I try to do the same thing, and I hope that when others see it, it will inspire them to pass it on as well — to be there for the people who need them. My kids, fortunately, seem to have learned this lesson without me. But I hope I can still be an example to them and help them along their journeys. To love them, support them, and help them be their best selves. To help them understand that their potential is infinite and that there are always more ways to do good.

An inheritance or legacy, of course, is not just about physical things. Legacy is what you leave others, how you make them feel, and no one can take that from them. It's not just the material stuff. Emotional legacy is what's important.

That's the legacy that I want to leave for them, for my friends, and for you, my reader. A legacy of healing, of growth, of support. A legacy of helping, of being there for the people around us when they need us, and of having people in our lives who are there for us when we need them.

And hopefully, a legacy of understanding that wherever you go and whatever you do...

You will always be Enough.

JAREK TADLA is a seasoned real estate investor and passionate advocate for mental health awareness. With over 30 years of experience in residential and commercial real estate investment, he has cultivated a portfolio spanning thousands of units globally. Originally from Poland, Jarek embarked on his journey to achieve the American Dream, recognizing that every role, from dishwasher to boss, played a pivotal part in his development.

As the owner-operator of Peoples Choice Apartments LLC, Jarek has grown his real estate empire to one of the largest singularly owned real estate holding entities without investor equity in the country. Over the years, he has remediated and renovated countless properties, not only improving financial performance but also enhancing the overall living conditions for his tenants, a problem Jarek frequently experienced when he immigrated in the 90s.

Beyond his professional accomplishments, Jarek is a fervent advocate for mental health awareness and support. Having navigated his own demons with depression, he shares his deeply personal journey to inspire hope and resilience. As a man who came from nothing and built a hugely successful company, Jarek struggled to understand how you can have "everything in the world but still feel alone, unworthy, and miserable."

Jarek believes the prevalence of poor mental health is a systematic epidemic that must be addressed more publicly, regardless of social status. A life-altering accident and COVID awakened his passion to write *Not Enoughness: The Gift and The Curse.*

Through motivational speaking, workshops, and one-on-one coaching, Jarek is on a mission to create a safe space for individuals to explore their challenges, find solace, and discover their inner strength. His lifelong goal is to help others overcome adversity, foster resilience, and create a community of support.